Talmud Israeli
Daf Yomi for US

מחברים דורות מפגישים עולמות
Connecting Generations Bringing Together Worlds

Talmud Israeli-Daf Yomi for US
Masechet Berachot

Meir Jakobsohn — **Founder & Editor-in-Chief**
Rabbi Avi Rath — Educational Director & Editor
Haim Freilicman — Chairman of the Board

Gal Naor — Chairman, Daf Yomi for US
Yael Schulman — Director, Daf Yomi for US

English Language Translation and Editing Team:

Rabbi Evan Hoffman

Amy Erani

Dr. Penny Stern

Layout and Design
Amy Erani

Illustrations
B. Hevlin

The Talmud Israeli project has been supported by

Many generations have found the way to connect to their Jewish heritage through the Talmud, which spans the generations and connects the *Torah she'bi'chtav (*written law) and the *Torah she'be'al peh* (oral law).

The compilation before you is another in a series that will contain all of the *Daf Yomi for US* selections in a particular masechet. This book represents an invitation and an opportunity for renewal to join one's fellow Jews in a unique learning endeavor.

The Talmud is thousands of years old and still, nothing compares to it as a source of Jewish wisdom, *halacha, agada,* thought, and *midrash.* Learning Talmud brings us back to the origins of our people as well as together with a friend, a *chevruta* (study partner) – and most importantly, with our children.

Talmud Israeli aids in the blossoming of the Jewish identity that exists in our generation. The *iyyun,* deep concentration, the learning, the experience, the consistency, and the delving into ancient worlds, on one hand; and the current, relevant worlds revealed through Talmud study, on the other hand, challenge the reader and set a high bar of Jewish engagement.

The effort invested in this undertaking, and the finished product is the result of the vision of Meir and Tzilit Jakobsohn, who view this enterprise as their educational and spiritual life's work. Their goal is to contribute to the entirety of the Jewish people. From these volumes of Talmud Israeli comes the empowerment of learners as well as the strengthening of the inter-generational bond, the invigoration of the family unit and community reinforcement.

Since those moments of glory, holiness and unity, more than 3,300 years ago, when an entire nation stood as one, at the foothills of Mount Sinai, in order to receive the Torah, we have yearned for Hashem to *chadesh yameinu ke'kedem,* "renew our days, as those of old."

May the volumes of Talmud Israeli – Daf Yomi for US help us to follow in the footsteps of the past, enable us to walk humbly and show us the way to a future in which we will march forward in hope.

B'tefilla u'b'simcha,
Avi Rath

The Jewish Talmud is a creation filled with wonder. It is ancient, stirring and delightful. Written in Babylonia and Jerusalem, the Talmud constitutes and remains the foundation stone of Jewish culture, halacha, and tradition.

More than a decade ago, in 2007, as former students and current parents, we thought about how to make the sugiyot of the Talmud accessible to readers in a manner that is both challenging and enjoyable. We recognized the importance of effectively accomplishing this goal, embracing the study of Talmud as an ingenious tool to transmit Jewish tradition from parents to children, for the sake of the continuity of our people.

Over the course of the past years, we have published a weekly study sheet, integrated with specially-selected segments to bring together the concepts of the Talmud sugiyot with Jewish history and values. In 2016, we began translating our material into English and are thrilled to offer our materials to learners in North America.

The Talmud Israeli volumes in Hebrew are the fulfillment of our dream. We envisioned a way to preserve and strengthen Talmudic tradition and we are honored that so many people around the world use our books each day. It is thrilling to realize the potential reach of our newest series in English. Our ultimate goal is to translate the entire series.

To fulfill this mission and succeed in satisfying and challenging the learners of our materials in a way that befits for the beauty and creativity of the Talmudic sugiyot, we decided to embark on a range of activities. Headed by Avi Rath, these efforts are bearing fruit as we continue to build learning centers throughout Israel and the world.

Shortly after welcoming in the new century, our mother and mother-in-law, **Navah Bar-El z"l** passed away suddenly. Savta Navah deeply appreciated the importance of "family togetherness" as the central value of a warm home. Therefore, we chose to commemorate and perpetuate her memory with Talmud Israeli, a project that reinforces the bond between parents and children. As such, the initial step in this project was to bring parents and children together in groups to enjoy shared learning.

This newest program, Talmud Israeli — Daf Yomi for US, is dedicated in loving memory to our father and father-in-law **Yehoshua (Shuki) Zipori z"l.** Saba Shuki loved to learn and was the epitome of an *'ish sefer'*, a lifelong scholar. We feel that the best way to honor Saba Shuki's memory is to broaden the project that meant so much to him and to expand the reach of Talmud Israeli through our new English language publications.

We are thankful to the *Ribono Shel Olam* for the great privilege of being partners in spreading Talmud learning and bringing its riches into the lives of Jewish families.

Tzilit & Meir Jakobsohn, Founders

We thank *HaKadosh Baruch Hu,* that *be'sha'ah tova,* we have completed another English language *Masechet* of the *Talmud Israeli — Daf Yomi for US.* We appreciate the trust and support of the Talmud Israeli founders, Meir and Tzilit Jakobsohn, who made the success of *Talmud Israeli-Daf Yomi for US* possible.

In recent months, dozens of institutions, both schools and synagogues, representing thousands of learners, have joined the *Talmud Israeli* family. Each facility has come to the study of Daf Yomi in its own way — some through special classes dedicated to utilizing Talmud Israeli, some in *chevrutot* or groups, and others with parent-child learning.

Talmud Israeli has made it possible for students who would otherwise not be exposed to these studies to join the world-wide pool of *Daf Yomi* learners. It has been a privilege to introduce these students to Daf Yomi and include them in Talmudic learning.

We thank Yael Schulman, who leads the project in North America, for all of her hard work in bringing Talmud Israeli to this new audience, adapting the materials for them, and ensuring continued success among a fresh group of enthusiastic learners.

Shlomit & Gal Naor

MASECHET
Berachot
[Selections From Daf Yomi]

פרק א'
מֵאֵימָתַי

מן התלמוד:
סדר זרעים
מסכת ברכות
דף ב'.

FROM THE TALMUD
SEDER ZERA'IM
MASECHET BERACHOT
DAF 2A

Translation

ראיה	... Re'ah'yah	Proof
זכר	... Zecher	Hint, allusion
צאת הכוכבים	... Tzeit Ha'Kochavim	Appearance of stars

Explanation

The *Gemara* asserts that the day ends and the next day begins when the stars appear in the sky. The *Gemara* concedes there is no absolute proof for this, but there is a hint to it in Scripture. Had there been evidence from the Torah, that would have constituted unquestionable proof. Since the actual citation is from *Ketuvim* (Book of Nechemiah) it serves merely as a hint, a lesser form of textual support.

"ואף על פי שאין ראיה לדבר זכר לדבר, שנאמר ואנחנו עושים במלאכה וחצים מחזיקים ברמחים מעלות השחר עד צאת הכוכבים, ואומר והיו לנו הלילה משמר והיום מלאכה".

מִצְוַת קְרִיאַת שְׁמַע
THE MITZVAH OF RECITING THE SHEMA YISRAEL PRAYER

On this first *daf* of *Masechet Berachot,* in the first *seder* (order) of the six *sedarim* in the Talmud, we learn about the *mitzvah* of *K'riyat Shema* (recitation of the Shema prayer). "*K'riyat Shema*" is the recitation of three Scriptural paragraphs, the first of which begins with the famous verse "*Shema Yisrael, HaShem Elo'key'nu, HaShem Echad*" (Hear O Israel, HaShem is our God, HaShem is One). Tradition calls on Jews to recite *K'riyat Shema* twice daily, once in the evening and once in the morning.

The evening *K'riyat Shema* may be recited as early as nightfall, identifiable when three stars appear in the sky. The window of opportunity to fulfill the mitzvah extends until the crack of dawn. However, *Chazal* (our sages) ruled that one best act quickly to fulfill the requirement of *K'riyat Shema* before the middle of the night. This rabbinic safeguard was enacted so that people not be negligent, inadvertently doze off, and consequently forget to recite *K'riyat Shema.*

שְׁמַע יִשְׂרָאֵל...

כִּנּוֹרוֹ שֶׁל דָּוִד הַמֶּלֶךְ
KING DAVID'S LYRE

The *Gemara* relates the words of Rabbi Shimon Chasida, who said that over the course of many years, King David would wake up at midnight and study the holy Torah.

In the absence of modern technology, how did King David know the exact moment of midnight? The *Gemara* says that King David hung a lyre over his bed. When midnight arrived, the northern wind would blow and cause the strings of the lyre to vibrate and play on their own. King David would hear the sound of the lyre music playing and immediately jump up to study Torah.

בִּרְכַּת הַגְּאֻלָּה
THE BLESSING OF REDEMPTION

On this *daf,* we learn about *Birkat HaGeulah* (the Blessing of Redemption). *Birkat HaGeulah* is the blessing, *"Baruch Atah HaShem, Ga'al Yisrael,"* in which we bless Hashem who redeemed our ancestors from Egypt.

After reciting *K'riyat Shema* in the morning and evening, the blessing *"Baruch Atah HaShem, Ga'al Yisrael"* is recited, immediately before the *Amidah* (standing) prayer. The *Gemara* rules that it is prohibited to pause for any reason (e.g., to speak) between reciting the *"Ga'al Yisrael"* blessing and the *Amidah* (also known as *"Shmoneh Esrei,"* eighteen blessing) prayer.

Why absolute silence essential at that juncture of the service? Because during the *tefillah (Amidah, Shemoneh Esrei)* one stands before the King of Kings, the Holy One Blessed is He. How should one behave when standing before a king? One praises the king and then makes an approach. After that, one submits various *bakashot* (requests). We too, praise the God for redeeming our people from Egypt and immediately after that, we offer the *Shemoneh Esrei* prayer in which we include our *bakashot.*

Once, the *Amora* Rav Huna suffered a great financial loss. He had 400 barrels of wine, all of which became fermented and turned to vinegar

When his friends, the other *Chachamim,* were informed of what had happened, they commented that when a person receives an *o'nesh miShamayim* (a Divine punishment), he must examine his actions to determine whether he has violated a prohibition and what he can do to rectify his behavior.

The *Chachamim* continued: "We heard you had a worker, an *a'rees* (tenant farmer) who tended to your grapevines, whom you did not pay the full share he deserved. Can you justify your actions?" Rav Huna explained that the worker had not been a decent, honest person and that numerous times, he took grapes from the vineyard without permission. Nevertheless, the *Chachamim* explained to Rav Huna that even though they believed his accusations against the worker to be true, he nonetheless needed to pay the worker his full salary.

According to the *Gemara,* Rava Huna heeded the advice of the *Chachamim.* He agreed to do as they said and paid the *a'rees* his full salary — after which, it appeared that a miracle had occurred. Some say Rav Huna's vinegar turned back into wine, and others say the price of vinegar rose until it was identical to the price of wine!

Translation

אין .... ay'n .... **Is not**

נשמעת .... nish'ma'at ..... **heard**

אלא .... elah .... **except for**

Explanation

Hashem can and does hear prayers regardless of the location from which those prayers were recited. Nonetheless, it is preferable (and one's prayers are more likely to be favorably heard) for one to pray in a synagogue, even if at an off hour when the congregation is not gathered for communal prayers.

מן התלמוד:
סדר זרעים
מסכת ברכות
דף ו.

"אבא בנימין אומר
אין תפילה של אדם נשמעת
אלא בבית הכנסת".

FROM THE TALMUD
SEDER ZERA'IM
MASECHET BERACHOT
DAF 6A

**DAF 6
ו'**

מָתַי צָרִיךְ לָרוּץ?
WHEN MUST ONE RUN TO ACT?

According to Rabbi Chelbo, Rav Huna stated: One who leaves a synagogue should walk slowly and in a relaxed manner. Moreover, one should not run or take long strides. For if an individual runs, it appears as if he or she did not really want to be in the synagogue.

On the other hand, when one approaches a synagogue, it is a *mitzvah* to show enthusiasm by rushing to get there.

The *Gemara* continues — although it is discouraged to rush and race on *Shabbat*, when one is heading to learn Torah or hear a *shiur,* speeding to fulfill the *mitzvah* of *limmud Torah* is encouraged. Rabbi Zeira initially thought the *Chachamim* were acting inappropriately when he saw them running to attend a Torah *shiur* on Shabbat. However, after Rabbi Zeira heard that one should always rush to hear a halachic discourse even on Shabbat, he himself began to run for such purposes as well.

כֹּחֶהּ שֶׁל תְּפִלַּת צִבּוּר
THE POWER OF PUBLIC PRAYER

The *Gemara* says that Rabbi Yitzchak asked Rabbi Nachman why he did not go to a *Beit K'nesset* to pray? Rabbi Nachman replied that he was sick and weak, and did not have the strength to get to the *shul.* In response, Rabbi Yitzchak inquired why Rabbi Nachman did not gather nine others to pray together in his home. Rabbi Nachman contended that gathering a *minyan* in his home was also beyond his ability.

Rabbi Yitzchak then told Rabbi Nachman: "If that is the case, then at least pray at the same time that the *minyan* prays in the synagogue!"

At which point, Rabbi Nachman questioned Rabbi Yitzchak: "Why are you making such a fuss about this matter?" Rabbi Yitzchak answered that Rabbi Shimon Bar Yochai maintained that even a person who is forced to pray at home alone — and not in a *minyan* — should pray at the same time the *minyan* prays in the synagogue, because the time when a *minyan* is in progress at the synagogue is an *et ratzon* ("time of favor"), when God hears the prayers of all who pray together.

שְׁנַיִם מִקְרָא וְאֶחָד תַּרְגּוּם
TWO TIMES IN HEBREW AND ONCE IN TRANSLATION

On this *daf* we learn the principle of *"Shnayim Mikra v'Echad Targum."* Rav Huna Bar Yehudah said in the name of Rav Ami that during the course of each week a person should read the entire *Parashat HaShavua* (weekly Torah portion) that will be read in synagogue on Shabbat.

The phrase *"Shnayim Mikra"* calls for reading *Parashat HaShavua* twice and *"Echad Targum"* requires one additional reading of the *Targum Onkelos,* which is a translation of the Torah text into Aramaic. In many printed chumshim, Targum Onkelos appears in a column next to the original Hebrew text of Torah. For those unfamiliar with Aramaic, it is appropriate to read a translation of the Parashah in one's own vernacular.

Weekly reading of *"Shnayim Mikra v'Echad Targum"* is a meritorious practice that may result in a lengthy life.

מִצְוָה לִרְאוֹת מְלָכִים
A MITZVAH TO SEE A KING

Rabbi Zeira was once forced to purchase a crown of myrtle branches as a gift for the king, as was the custom of his time. Rabbi Zeira regretted his obligation to spend money for the purchase of the myrtle branches, which he felt was a waste of his resources. Rabbi Yossi Ben Elyakim heard Rabbi Zeira complain and told him he need not be sorry about the expense, since he was fulfilling a *mitzvah.* Even if he had not been forced into purchasing the gift, it would have been incumbent upon him to expend resources to catch a glimpse of the king.

In what way is it virtuous, and hence obligatory, to see a heathen monarch? Rabbi Yochanan explained that it is a *mitzvah* to greet a king, even one from other nations, so that in the future, at the time of full redemption, it will be proven that the greatest honor was bestowed upon the King of Israel.

לְהַצְמִיד אֶת הָרַגְלַיִם בַּתְּפִלָּה
PLACING ONE'S LEGS TOGETHER IN PRAYER

Rabbi Yossi son of Rabbi Hanina shared several *halachot* taught by Rabbi Eliezer Ben Ya'akov:

Halacha #1:
When praying, one should stand in a topographically low place rather than in an elevated location, as suggested in the words of the verse: "From the depths I call out to you, *HaShem*" (Psalms 30:1) — i.e., from a deep, or low place I pray to you, God.

Halacha #2:
While reciting the *Amidah* prayer, one should keep their legs straight and place both feet together, aligning them one next to the other. The *Gemara* states that an individual who stands in prayer with straightened legs and both feet together, as one, is likened to the angels, regarding whom it was said in the Book of Ezekiel (1:7) "And their feet were one straight foot." Meaning, their legs remained close to each other and had the appearance of being one leg.

Halacha #3:
It is prohibited to eat
before the *Shacharit* (morning) prayers.

בִּרְכוֹת הַתּוֹרָה לִפְנֵי הַתְּפִלָּה
TORAH BLESSINGS BEFORE THE CORE PRAYER SERVICE

Rav Yehudah taught in the name of Shmuel that one should not begin to study Torah before reciting the Torah blessings: *"Baruch Atah, HaShem… v'Tzivanu la'asok b'divrei Torah"* (Blessed are You, God … who has commanded us to engage in matters of Torah.) *"V'ha'arev na HaShem Elo'key'nu [et divrei Toratecha b'phee'nu] … Baruch Atah HaShem … Noten HaTorah"* (Please sweeten, HaShem, our God [the words of Your Torah in our mouths] … Blessed are You, HaShem … Giver of the Torah).

Nevertheless, the *Gemara* adds, if an individual completes recitation of the *Shacharit* prayers and afterward recalls having forgotten to recite the Torah blessings, it is not necessary to go back and recite the. Why not? Because among the blessings associated with *K'riyat Shema* is the blessing of *"Ahava Rabbah"* (great love) which incorporates requests to God that He help us to learn and understand Torah. This serves the same purpose as the formal Torah blessings.

מן התלמוד:
סדר זרעים
מסכת ברכות
דף י"ב.

FROM THE TALMUD
SEDER ZERA'IM
MASECHET BERACHOT
DAF 12A

"אַף בַּגְּבוּלִין בִּקְשׁוּ לִקְרוֹת
כֵּן אֶלָּא שֶׁכְּבָר בִּטְּלוּם מִפְּנֵי
תַּרְעוֹמֶת הַמִּינִין".

Translation

גְּבוּלִין .... *Gevulin* .... **Outlying areas**

מִינִין .... *Minin* .... **Heretics**

Explanation

The reading of the Ten Commandments was part of the liturgy in the Holy Temple. The sages attempted to include it in the synagogue liturgy as part of Kriyat Shema. But the suggestion was rejected so as not to give support to sectarian heretics who claimed that only the Ten Commandments (and not the rest of the Torah) is true.

DAF 12
י"ב

כָּךְ כּוֹרְעִים בִּתְפִלַּת הָעֲמִידָה
THIS IS HOW ONE BOWS DURING THE AMIDAH PRAYER

It is obligatory to bend one's knees and bow several times during the recitation of the *Amidah* prayer. One bows at the beginning of the first *bracha* (blessing) of the *Amidah*, while reciting *"Baruch Atah HaShem …,"* and the end of that *bracha* *"Baruch Atah HaShem … [Magen Avraham],"* as well as at the beginning and end of the Thanksgiving (*Modim*) blessing.

In the *Gemara,* we learn that Rabba Bar Hinana Sava said in the name of Rav: When one recites: *"Baruch Atah HaShem",* one should bow as they recite the word *"Baruch"* (Blessed) and then subsequently stand straight and upright when reciting *"HaShem,"* God's name.

The *Gemara* also relates that Rav Sheshet would bow quickly, in one smooth motion. Though when he began to stand upright, he would lift himself up slowly, with great patience. First, Rav Sheshet would lift his head and then his body. Why did he do this? So that no one would think he stood because it was too difficult for him to continue bowing, and to demonstrate his love and awe of Hashem. Thus, Rav Sheshet would take his time returning to a standing position.

בָּרוּךְ אַתָּה ה'

'אַבְרָהָם' וְ'אַבְרָם'
'AVRAHAM' AND 'AVRAM'

The names of two of our holy patriarchs were changed. When *Avraham Avinu* of blessed memory was born, they called him *"Avram,"* (without the letter *"Hey"*). It was only later on that Hashem added the letter *"Hey"* to his name. From that time on, he was known only as *"Avraham."*

The name of *Ya'akov Avinu* of blessed memory was also changed. At first, he was called "Ya'akov." After he struggled with Esav's ministering angel and emerged victorious, the angel informed him that God would change his name from 'Ya'akov' to 'Yisrael'.

However, there is a distinction between the name transformation of *Avraham Avinu* and that of *Ya'akov Avinu*. *Avraham Avinu's* name was replaced and instead of 'Avram' he was to be called 'Avraham'. From that time onward, it was forbidden to refer to *Avraham Avinu* as 'Avram,' because his proper, true name became 'Avraham.' In contrast, the name of *Ya'akov Avinu* was not truly replaced. Rather, a name was added to his birth name, and from that day on, he was called both Ya'akov and Yisrael.

כָּךְ נַתְחִיל אֶת הַיּוֹם
THE WAY TO BEGIN THE DAY

Rav and Shmuel taught that prior to reciting the *Shacharit* prayer service, one is not to go to the home of a fellow to greet them. If, however, one unexpectedly runs into a friend or acquaintance on the street, it is permitted to ask how that person is doing and extend a friendly greeting.

Rav Idi Bar Abin said in the name of Rav Yitzchak Bar Ashyan that one should not attend to any of their personal affairs before morning *tefilla*. The *Gemara* adds that Hashem aids and helps satisfy the wishes of those who pray before setting out on their way.

On this *daf,* we learn from Rabbi Yochanan that a Jew who learns a significant amount of Torah before going to sleep need not fear having a head filled with bad tidings. Rabbi Yochanan derived this teaching from a verse in *Mishlei* (Proverbs 19:23), "and he will sleep satiated (filled), and will not be visited by evil" — meaning, one who goes to sleep satiated by teachings of the Torah will not be visited by bad dreams.

On this *daf,* Rav Ovadia cites a *braita* (Tannaitic teaching) stating that *K'riyat Shema* is to be recited in its entirety, without omitting anything. However, it is also important to pause between certain words -- i.e., those which when recited too quickly, are difficult to enunciate each of their letters clearly.

Rava provides examples of words that require a separation between them. In the Kriyat Shema we say: "*V'hayu had'varim ha'eleh ... ahl levavecha*". If the words "*ahl levavecha*" are said to quickly, they sound like one word, "*a'levavecha*" instead of "*ahl levavecha*" Therefore, it is necessary to recite "*ahl*" distinctively and serenely, without any hurry, and then continue with "*levavecha.*" Such exactitude results in the proper fulfilment of the mitzvah of *K'riyat Shema.*

The *Gemara* states that laborers who agreed to work the entire day for a contractor are not to recite all of the *brachot* (blessings) of *Birkat HaMazon* (Grace After Meals). Rather, they must skip over a portion of the *brachot* — for if they were to recite all of the *brachot* in *Birkat HaMazon,* they would be unable to work during that time, and the employer would lose money by paying them for time they were not working.

Which *brachot* should full-day laborers skip? Full-day laborers are not to recite the *brachot* obligated by rabbinic law. However, they are required to recite the *brachot* mandated by the Torah. Therefore, after the laborers finish eating, they recite the first *bracha* of *Birkat HaMazon*: "*Baruch Atah HaShem, Elo-heynu Melech ha'olam, Ha'zahn et ha'olam...*" (Blessed are You *HaShem,* our God, Ruler of the universe, who sustains the entire world...). After that, it is sufficient for the laborers to recite one additional *bracha,* which is an abridged version of the "*Nodeh Lecha*" (We Thank You) and the "*Rechem Na*" (Have mercy) — and more than that they do not say.

פרק ג'
מִי שֶׁמֵּתוֹ

Translation

פוק ... Pook .... **Go out**

חזי ... Chazi .... **See**

בטלני ... Idle, out of work ... **Idle, out of work**

איכא .... Ee'ka .... **There are**

Explanation

Rabban Shimon ben Gamliel suggested that common people comport themselves like Torah scholars and not work on Tisha b'Av. He did not regard this as a display of haughtiness, because onlookers will simply assume that the idle individual is unemployed as are many other people loitering in the marketplace.

FROM THE TALMUD
SEDER ZERA'IM
MASECHET BERACHOT
DAF 17B

מן התלמוד:
סדר זרעים
מסכת ברכות
דף י״ז:

"הרואה
אומר
מלאכה הוא דאין לו
פוק חזי
כמה בטלני
איכא בשוקא".

DAF 17
י״ז

תְּפִלָּה פְּרָטִית אַחֲרֵי הַתְּפִלָּה
PRIVATE PRAYER FOLLOWING THE AMIDAH

The final *bracha* (blessing) of the *Amidah* prayer is *"Sim shalom tova u'vracha"* (Grant peace, goodness and blessing [everywhere]). Following the recitation of *"Sim Shalom,"* it is acceptable for an individual to pray for things that are personally important to them, using whatever words they so choose.

The *Gemara* shares a few personal post-Amidah prayers composed by individual *Amoraim*. Rav supplemented his statutory prayer with a supplication that we customarily recite on *Shabbat Mevarchim* in preparation for and recognition the upcoming new month: *"Yehi ratzon Mil'fa'necha, she'Tee'ten lanu chayim aru'kim, chayim shel shalom..."* (May it be Your will, that You grant us long life, a life of peace...). When Mar bar Ravina concluded his *Amidah* prayers he said: *"Elo-hai netzor leshoni meh'ra"* (My God, guard my tongue from evil), which is popularly recited after *"Sim Shalom"* even today.

The *Gemara* continues and says that Rav Safra also prayed for all those who study the holy Torah that they may be privileged to learn *"L'shem Shamayim"* — (for the sake of Heaven, i.e., for the right reasons).

Benayahu son of Yehoyada was head of the *Sanhedrin* (High Court) during the reign of King David.

The *Navi* (prophet) called Benayahu by the name *"M'Kav'tze'el."* *Chazal* explained that Benayahu was given that nickname (from the root *'mekabetz'*, i.e., to gather), as he had gathered and amassed many learners to increase the study of Torah. Benayahu worked tirelessly so that a great number of Jews would be able to assemble in public and learn the sacred Torah.

The *Gemara* teaches that Benayahu was a tremendously wise and exalted Torah scholar, so much so that it was said there was no *talmid chacham* who matched Benayahu's level of knowledge and scholarship during the entire period of both the First and Second Holy Temples.

Benayahu would diligently engage in the study of Torah. On one occasion, it was exceptionally cold and an enormous amount of snow fell. However, Benayahu paid no attention to the weather. Instead, he spent the whole day eagerly studying the entire *"Sifra d'Bei Rav,"* a collection of halachic expositions on *Sefer VaYikra* (Book of Leviticus).

DOES DADDY KNOW?

The Gemara asks an almost unanswerable question: Do the dead know what is happening to the living here on earth? The sons of Rabbi Hiyya left the academy for a significant length of time to attend to their estates in the village. Being away from the *Beit Midrash*, they forgot their Torah studies and were very aggrieved. They asked each other whether their father was aware of their emotional distress. Their initial thought was that their father was unaware and they cited a verse from the Book of Iyov (14:21):

"His sons may attain honor and he will not know it."

"She'at'nez" is the term used to describe a garment made from both wool and linen. It is prohibited to wear such clothing — as is written in *Sefer Devarim* 22:11 (Book of Deuteronomy): "You shall not wear *'She'at'nez,'* wool and linen combined together."

The *Gemara* states that if a Jew discovers he is wearing a *She'at'nez* garment, he should remove it immediately, even if doing so causes embarrassment and the need to remain without that garment in public, since the fulfillment of *mitzvot* has utmost importance and value.

It is only regarding the *mitzvah* of *Hashavat Aveidah* (returning a lost object) that there is an exception made. If an individual is embarrassed to handle an *aveidah* (lost object), that person is *patur* (exempt) from having to fulfill the *mitzvah* in that specific instance. Customarily, when a person finds an *aveidah*, the finder is required to pick up the object. However, if a distinguished individual finds an *aveidah* and is too embarrassed to handle the lost item they found, the distinguished individual is *patur* from handling it. For example, if a *talmid chacham* (Torah scholar) walked in the street and saw a lost sheep, that *talmid chacham* is not required to take the sheep and declare the *metzia* (found item) — since the *talmid chacham* would be embarrassed to lead an animal through the street. Evidence for this assertion is that if the sheep belonged to the *talmid chacham* himself, likely he would not personally handle the animal in public.

In this *sugiya* (Talmudic discussion), a new concept is raised and clarified: *"Mitzvat Aseh She'ha'zman Gerama"* (positive time-bound commandments). There are some *mitzvot* that may be fulfilled at any time, e.g., the *mitzvah* of giving *tzedakah*. If a person sees a needy individual in the morning, s/he can give that person *tzedakah* — and if a person sees a needy individual in the afternoon, s/he can also give that person *tzedakah* — and if a person sees a needy individual in the middle of the night, s/he can give that person *tzedakah*.

In contrast, there are other *mitzvot* that are not always possible to fulfill. The *mitzvah* of *K'riyat Shema,* for example, is not possible to fulfill throughout the day. There is a set window of opportunity to recite *K'riyat Shema* in the morning (*"u'v'kumecha,"* when you rise up). One who neglects to do so cannot fulfill the mitzvah later that afternoon.

Once the concept of *"Mitzvat Aseh she'ha'zman Gerama,"*— i.e., that there are positive commandments whose performance must be fulfilled during a fixed time — is understood, it is possible to continue with the lesson of this *Gemara*. This *Gemara* notes a general exemption for women from *Mitzvot Aseh She'ha'zman Gerama.* And if one were to question why women are, nevertheless, obligated to pray — as the *Shacharit* service may only be prayed in the morning and *Mincha* from the afternoon until the evening — therefore, why isn't *tefillah* considered a *Mitzvat She'ha'zman Gerama?*

The *Gemara* explains that even though the *mitzvah* of *tefillah* only remains in effect at particular times, the *Chachamim* still ruled women should pray every day, since it is during *tefillah* that we ask for mercy and make *bakashot* (requests) of Hashem.

WOMEN AND KIDDUSH

Rav Ada bar Ahavah ruled that women are obligated in the mitzvah of kiddush on Shabbat. The Gemara questioned this ruling on the grounds that the recitation of kiddush is a positive time-bound commandment, a category of mitzvah for which women are generally exempt. Answer: The Torah commands that we "remember" (zachor) and "safeguard" (shamor) the Sabbath. The two aspects of Sabbath observance were uttered simultaneously by Hashem, and whomever is obligated in latter is necessarily also obligated in the former. Since woman are generally obligated in all prohibitive commandments, including the ban on Sabbath work, they are also obligated in the performative aspects of the Sabbath, notably reciting kiddush.

הַטּוֹעֶה בַּתְּפִלָּה
A MISTAKENLY-RECITED PRAYER

What should be done by an individual who began to recite the *Amidah* prayer and suddenly remembered — in the middle of the prayer — that he had already prayed?

The *Gemara* relates the words of Shmuel who taught that in the aforementioned case, one should immediately stop recitation of the *Amidah,* even in the middle of a blessing, since that prayer is unnecessary and redundant.

The weekday *Amidah* contains 19 blessings (as will be elaborated upon in *daf* 28), while the *Amidah* prayers for Shabbat are shorter and each consists of only seven blessings. The *Gemara* asks what a person should do if, on Shabbat, instead of reciting the *Amidah* for Shabbat, s/he mistakenly recited the *Tefillat Amidah* for weekdays. Should s/he stop in the middle of whatever blessing he or she was reciting?!

In response, the *Gemara* concludes that this individual should not stop in the middle of a blessing, but rather complete that particular blessing and then begin the proper *tefillah* for Shabbat. If, for example, an individual remembers that it is now Shabbat while in the middle of reciting the *"Hashiveinu Avinu l'Toratecha"* (Return us, our Father to Your Torah) blessing, s/he should not stop immediately, but rather finish reciting that blessing, *"Baruch Atah HaShem, HaRotzeh b'teshuvah"* (Blessed are You, *HaShem,* who desires our return) — and only then begin to recite the appropriate Shabbat prayers.

לִמּוּד תּוֹרָה בְּכֹבֶד רֹאשׁ
LEARNING TORAH AMID SERIOUS DISTRACTION

Several different matters are discussed on this *daf,* including:

1. One must study Torah with a serious mindset and without indulging in levity, just as the Nation of Israel stood at Mount Sinai and received the Torah in a state of reverence and trepidation before God.

2. There are certain *mitzvot* that may be fulfilled only in *Eretz Yisrael,* such as the *mitzvah* of *Shmittah* (the Sabbatical year); the *mitzvah* of *Terumah* (priestly gifts); and other *mitzvot* which are called *"Mitzvot ha't'luyot ba'Aretz"* (commandments tied to the Land), since their fulfillment is tied to one's presence in *Eretz Yisrael.*

The Tannaim debated whether the *mitzvah* of *Reisheet HaGez* (which mandates that a Jew who owns and shears sheep is required to give a portion of the wool to the *kohen*) was a *Mitzvah ha't'luya ba'Aretz,* one which should only be fulfilled in *Eretz Yisrael,* or whether the law is applicable in *Chutz l'Aretz* (outside of *Eretz Yisrael*) as well. Rambam ruled that the law only applies in *Eretz Yisrael.*

3. It is prohibited to pray in an unclean location. A prayer recited in such a place is invalid and whomever recited it would then need to pray once again in an appropriate place.

שֶׁקִּית הַתְּפִלִּין
THE *TEFILLIN* BAG

Ritual objects containing the Divine Name, like a *Sefer Torah, Mezuzah,* and *Tefillin,* are sacred. Rav Hisda added that not only are the *Tefillin* themselves holy, but the bag in which one places the *Tefillin* is holy as well. Therefore, it is prohibited to put money, or any other item in a *Tefillin* bag. However, if the owner of the bag does not intend to use it for *Tefillin* on a permanent basis, rather just temporarily, then the bag may also be used for other purposes.

Moreover, if an individual prepared a new bag for *Tefillin,* to be used on a regular basis, but had not yet started to place *Tefillin* inside it, that bag may be used to hold other items, until the *Tefillin* are placed inside the bag.

In summary: In order for a *Tefillin* bag to become prohibited for other uses, two conditions must be in place: 1) the bag must be a special bag designated for holding *Tefillin* on a regular basis; 2) the bag must already be in use for the purpose of holding *Tefillin.*

כָּךְ מִתְפַּלְלִים אֶת תְּפִלַּת הָעֲמִידָה
THIS IS HOW THE AMIDAH PRAYER IS RECITED

It says in the *Gemara* that the *Amidah* prayer should not be recited out loud, because doing so seems as if one does not believe God can hear whispered prayers.

Rav Huna says that only if an individual is able to pray in a whisper and maintain the proper focus and intention, should s/he pray quietly. However, if it is too difficult to concentrate on prayer, one is permitted to pray out loud. These instances refer to cases when an individual prays alone. However, when an individual prays among other people (*b'tzibur,* in a prayer community), it is prohibited to recite the *Amidah* out loud, lest one person's prayer disrupt the ability of the rest of the congregation to maintain the required level of focus and concentration.

In this *sugiya* (Talmudic discussion), we learned about the prohibition against thinking about matters of Torah, or praying, or reciting *K'riyat Shema* in a filthy location. One is also prohibited from reciting *K'riyat Shema* in a place with a bad odor; one must move away from the source of the odor and only then recite *K'riyat Shema*.

הָאֶצְבַּע הַמִּתְפַּלֶּלֶת
THE FINGER THAT PRAYS

The *Gemara* discusses an interesting question on this *daf*. Previously we learned that it is prohibited to pray in a filthy location. Here, the *Gemara* relates a *machloket* (debate) about an individual who stood in a clean location but put a finger into a filthy spot. Is such a person permitted to recite *K'riyat Shema?*

On one hand, the individual's finger is in no way involved in the recitation of *K'riyat Shema,* it is only his or her mouth. If that is the case, it should theoretically be permissible for the individual to recite *K'riyat Shema!* On the other hand, it says in *Tehillim* (Psalms 35:10): *"Kol atzmo'tai to'mar'na"* (All my bones shall say) — in other words, the entire body is a partner in prayer, the finger as well. So, arguably, it should be forbidden to pray even if just one finger is in a dirty location. The halachah accords with the lenient view.

On this daf, the Gemara discusses *"Vatikin."* They were people who love performing *mitzvot*. The *Vatikin* would arise early in the morning to recite K'riyat Shema, which they would juxtapose with the recitation of the Amidah. The latter would be commenced by the Vatikin at the precise moment of sunrise, the earliest permitted moment for doing so.

TEFILLIN IN THE BATHROOM

If one is in the synagogue and needs to use the restroom, one should remove *Tallit* and *Tefillin* before entering the restroom. But what if that is not option. For example, if while travelling one needs to use the restroom but cannot find a safe place temporarily to store the *Tefillin?* (This is a common occurrence at airports, where it is unacceptable to leave packages unattended.) Under such conditions, the concerns about theft or sacrilege override the preference to keep *Tefillin* out of an unclean place. Therefore, one should bring the *Tefillin* into the restroom, but first put them inside a bag which is itself inside one's luggage.

תְּפִלַת הַשַּׁחַר

פרק ד'

תְּפִלַת תַּשְׁלוּמִין
MAKING UP FOR MISSED PRAYERS

Jewish law calls for the recitation of three daily prayer services. In the morning — *Shacharit;* in the afternoon — *Mincha;* in the evening— *Arvit.*

What should one do to compensate for prayers one did not recite?

The *Gemara* says that missed prayer can be made up at the following time for prayer — e.g., a person who had not recited the *Shacharit Amidah* in the morning may recite the *Mincha Amidah* twice in the afternoon; a person who had not recited the *Mincha Amidah* in the afternoon may recite the *Arvit Amidah* twice in the evening. The second recitation of the *Amidah* is called a *"Tefillat Tashlumin"* (a compensatory, or "makeup" prayer), because it is recited to compensate for the prayer that was missed.

Not every individual is permitted to recite *Tefillat Tashlumin.* Only one who missed reciting prayers through no fault of his own is entitled to recite the compensatory prayer. However, one who willfully neglected to pray forfeits the opportunity to fulfill that *mitzvah.* As King Solomon said in *Kohelet* (Ecclesiastes 1:15): "What is crooked cannot be made straight."

Translation

נוקמיה ... *Nokimei* .... **Let us establish**
חכם ... *Chacham* .... **Wise**
עשיר ... *Asheer* .... **Wealthy**
עשירי ... *Ah'see'ree*........ **Tenth generation**

Explanation

When Rabban Gamliel was deposed, it was suggested that Rabbi Elazar ben Azariah be appointed as his replacement. He was extremely qualified in that he was scholarly, wealthy, and of illustrious pedigree (tenth generation descendant from Ezra).

מן התלמוד:
סדר זרעים
מסכת ברכות
דף כ״ז:

״נוקמיה
לרבי אלעזר בן עזריה
דהוא חכם והוא עשיר
והוא עשירי לעזרא״.

FROM THE TALMUD
SEDER ZERA'IM
MASECHET BERACHOT
DAF 27B

DAF 27 / כ״ז

תָּדִיר וְשֶׁאֵינוֹ תָּדִיר
FREQUENT AND INFREQUENT

In this *sugiya* (Talmudic discussion), the *Gemara* teaches a very important principle: "*Tadir v'she'ayno tadir — tadir kodem*" ([When there is] a frequent [action, *mitzvah*, occurrence] and an infrequent [action, *mitzvah*, occurrence] — the frequent [is performed] first."

The conventional sequence on Shabbat is: *Shacharit*, Torah reading, additional *Musaf* service, Shabbat Feast, and finally the afternoon *Mincha* service.

The *Gemara* discusses a case of someone who was unable to recite the additional *Musaf* prayer until the afternoon hours. By that point it is already permissible to recite the afternoon *Mincha* prayer. Which prayer service, then, should get preference — *Musaf* or *Mincha*?

The *Gemara* answers that *Mincha* should precede *Musaf*, because "*Tadir v'she'ayno tadir — tadir kodem*." Meaning, something that is done frequently should be done before something that is done infrequently. Since the *Mincha* prayers are recited each day, it is "*tadir*" (frequent); whereas *Musaf* is recited only on Shabbat and holidays, so it is "*ayna tadira*" (infrequent).

תְּפִלָּה לִפְנֵי לִמּוּד הַתּוֹרָה הַקְּדוֹשָׁה
PRAYER BEFORE LEARNING TORAH

Before learning Torah, a prayer is recited asking God for the ability to learn and properly comprehend Torah correctly and not to fail or err, Heaven forbid, in understanding the material.

Upon completion of a session of Torah study, another prayer is recited thanking God, Giver of the Torah, for the privilege of learning the Holy Book, through which one's destiny is fulfilled. "One gets up in the morning to learn Torah, walks in order to learn Torah, as is expected by Hashem. For this one merits great reward, because Torah study is itself the greatest gift in the world." The aforementioned words were composed by Rabbi Nehuniah Ben HaKaneh.

Regarding the 'Shmoneh Esrei' prayer: The Gemara notes that the number of brachot in the weekday Amidah is 19. Despite that fact, it is still called the Shmoneh Esrei (18). Why isn't this prayer referred to as the "Tesha Esrei" (19)? The Gemara explains that the Weekday Amidah initially was composed of just 18 blessings, and was hence named the "Shmoneh Esrei." Sometime later, Shmuel HaKatan (Samuel the Small), so named because he was extremely humble and not at all conceited, instituted an additional bracha "v'laMalshinim ahl te'hee tikvah" (and for the slanderers, let there be no hope). However, the original name of Shmoneh Esrei has been retained, a holdover from the days when the prayer indeed had just 18 blessings.

טָעֻיּוֹת בַּתְּפִלָּה
ERRORS IN PRAYER

Requires repetition: "V'ten tahl u'matar" — Recited during the winter months — If one forgets to add this bakasha (request) while reciting the birkat hashanim (#9), but remembers before reciting "Shema koleinu," (#16), then the "V'ten tahl u'matar" may be inserted within the Shema Koleinu blessing — before the chatima (closing portion of the blessing) "Ki Atah Sho'me'a" (because You hear…). Though, if the error only becomes evident after "Shema koleinu" has been recited, then it is necessary to go back to recite the Amidah again from "Barech aleinu" onward. In the event, it is not until after reciting the entire Amidah that the error was noticed, the person praying should repeat the entire Shemoneh Esrei prayer from the beginning.

Requires no repetition: "Atah Chonantanu" (You granted us knowledge): During the evening Arvit service on Motzei (conclusion of) Shabbat, we add the prayer "Atah Chonantanu" to the "Atah Chonen" (You bestow wisdom) blessing. The recitation of "Atah Chonantanu" serves to separate between the holy Shabbat and the remainder of the week, as in this prayer, it says: "Va'tavdel HaShem, Elokeinu bein kodesh l'chol … bein Yom HaSh'vi'I l'sheshet yemai ha'ma'aseh…" (And HaShem, our God distinguished between holy and mundane … between the seventh day and the six days of labor…"). If one forgets to say this liturgical insertion, it is not required to repeat the Amidah — since while reciting Havdalah over a cup of wine the separation between kodesh and chol is marked in a specially dedicated bracha — "HaMavdil bein kodesh l'chol" (Who distinguishes between holy and mundane).

תְּפִלַּת הַדֶּרֶךְ
TRAVELLER'S PRAYER

There is a prayer to recite when one heads out to travel: *"Yehi ratzon milfanecha HaShem … she'to'lee'cheinu l'shalom v'tatz'eedeinu l'shalom …"* (May it be Your will *HaShem* that You guide us in peace and lead us in peace…), as a request for safe passage throughout one's journey.

Not every excursion requires a designated prayer. Taking a short trip from one's home would not call for recitation of *Tefillat HaDerech*. In Talmudic times, when the roads were unsafe and before the advent of modern means of transportation, the blessing was mandated for journeys longer than a *parsah* (one parsang; 4 kilometers; 2.5 miles).

In examining the wording of the prayer, one would see that the *Chachamim* formulated *Tefillat HaDerech* in the plural form — *"she'to'lee'cheinu l'shalom v'tatz'eedeinu l'shalom."* Why shouldn't an individual who travels alone recite: "*… she'to'lee'che***ini** *l'shalom v'tatz'eede***ini** *l'shalom* (i.e., Who guides **me** in peace and leads **me** in peace)? The *Gemara* explains that the *Chachamim* instituted recitation of *Tefillat HaDerech* in the plural form, so that the *zechut* (merit, benefit) of other people travelling throughout the world at that same time would be attributed to the individual reciting the prayer. The merit of the community makes an individual's supplication more readily accepted.

תְּפִלָּה בְּשִׂמְחָה
JOY IN PRAYER

When a Jew prays, there is cause to rejoice in the fulfillment a *mitzvah*; namely, the privilege to worship God through prayer. Prayer is not to be engaged in out of sorrow, exhaustion, or lightheartedness. For this reason, the *Chachamim* incorporated *geulat mitzrayim* (redemption from Egypt) in both the evening and morning services immediately (or nearly so) preceding the Amidah. According to Rashi, the *Chachamim* instituted the recitation of *"Ashrei"* ("Happy" are those who dwell in Your house) in the afternoon service, because those verses contain words of praise that elevate the soul of the supplicant and cause them to be joyful.

Furthermore, the *Gemara* adds that from Hannah's prayer, which appears at the beginning of *Sefer Shmuel,* we learn many *halachot* regarding *tefillah.* For example:

Quiet prayer: The *Amidah (Shemoneh Esrei)* prayer is to be recited silently, the same way Hannah prayed quietly, in a soundless whisper.

An intoxicated individual: One who consumed an alcoholic beverage and became intoxicated is forbidden to pray. We derive this teaching from the actions of Eli the High Priest who mistakenly thought that Hannah was intoxicated. He rebuked her — saying: "Why are you praying while being drunk? That is forbidden. One may not stand before a King in such a state."

זֶה הַיּוֹם
עָשָׂה ה׳
נָגִילָה
וְנִשְׂמְחָה בוֹ

דִּבּוּר עִם הַקָּדוֹשׁ בָּרוּךְ הוּא
SPEAKING TO GOD

Once, a righteous Jew was out on a walk and stopped on the way to pray. Just then, a non-Jewish government Minister passed by and greeted the Jew with *"Shalom."* The Jew did not respond. The Minister got angry, and when the Jew finished praying the Minister reprimanded him — "Why didn't you answer me? I could have had you killed!"

The Jew replied: "Your honor, the Minister! Imagine that you were standing and conversing with your king, when at the same time, a friend passed by and greeted you, saying 'hi'. Would you stop talking to your king and respond to your friend's greeting?"

"Certainly, not!" the Minister replied.

"And had you chosen to stop speaking with the king, what would be done to you?" the Jew inquired.

"The king would have instructed them to hand me my head," the Minister admitted.

"So, sir," said the Jew, "you now understand?!" *Hashem* is the King of Kings. How could you want me to stop praying to Him in order to speak with you?

The Minister understood and peacefully dismissed the pious Jew.

הַבְדָּלָה בְּמוֹצָאֵי שַׁבָּת — פַּעֲמַיִם
HAVDALAH AT THE CONCLUSION OF SHABBAT — TWICE

On *Motzei* (the conclusion of) Shabbat, we mark the distinction between *kodesh* (holy) and *chol* (mundane, or ordinary) — meaning, we distinguish or separate between Shabbat and the remainder of the week.

The *Gemara* states that two *havdalot* (prayers of separation) are recited. The first *havdalah* is recited in the *Amidah* prayer during *Arvit shel Motzei Shabbat* (Saturday evening service), and the second *havdalah* is said at home in conjunction with blessings over wine, fragrant spices, and the light of the candle.

One who forgot to recite the first *havdalah* is not required to go back and repeat the entire *Amidah*, as after the *Arvit* service, the second *havdalah* is said. However, if one forgot to recite *havdalah* in the *Amidah* and also unlawfully ate food before reciting the second *havdalah* with the wine, spices and candle, then it is necessary to repeat the entire *Amidah* from the beginning.

Why? The *Chachamim* established this law as a *k'nas* (fine, penalty) for forgetting too many things that should not be forgotten.

Translation

עובר לפני התיבה ... *Oh'vehr lifnei ha'tey'vah* ... **Pass before the Ark (to serve as prayer leader)**

לסרב ... *Le'sah'rev* ... **Refuse**

דומה ... *Domeh* ... **Likened to**

שאין בו מלח ... *She'ayn bo melach* ... **That lacks salt**

תלמוד ישראלי
☆ *Daf Yomi For US*

FROM THE TALMUD
SEDER ZERA'IM
MASECHET BERACHOT
DAF 34A

מן התלמוד:
סדר זרעים
מסכת ברכות
דף ל״ד.

"העובר לפני התיבה
צריך לסרב
ואם אינו מסרב
דומה לתבשיל
שאין בו מלח".

Explanation

As a matter of humility, one who is asked to lead the congregation in prayer should at first refuse. Only upon the third request should he make his way toward the *Amud*. One who jumps to lead the service without hesitation is likened to a cooked dish lacking salt.

כְּרִיעוֹת בִּתְפִלַּת הָעֲמִידָה
BOWING DURING THE AMIDAH PRAYER

DAF 34
ל״ד

There are four points in the *Amidah* prayer where one is supposed to bow —

1) Beginning of the first *bracha* (blessing).

2) End of the first *bracha*.

3) Beginning of the *"Modim"* blessing.

4) End of the *"Modim"* blessing (at *"Baruch Atah ... HaTov Shim'cha u'Lecha na'eh l'hodot"* [Blessed are You ... Whose Name is Good and to Whom it is [only] fitting to give thanks]).

One who prays is not to bow during the *Amidah* other than at those four places as set forth by the *Chachamim*. The aforementioned ruling refers to regular individuals; however, the *Kohen Gadol* bowed at the beginning of each *bracha* in the *Amidah* and a king was to pray the entire *Amidah* in a bowing posture.

Why were the *Kohen Gadol* and king expected to bow more frequently than regular laymen? Because the more august the status of an individual, the more he must humble himself before God.

פרק ו'
כֵּיצַד מְבָרְכִין

DAF 35
ל"ה

בְּרָכָה לִפְנֵי הָאֹכֶל
BLESSING BEFORE EATING

The *Gemara* says one should not derive pleasure from this world without first reciting a *bracha* (blessing). For that reason, a Jew should learn the *halachot* pertaining to *brachot,* so as to know which *bracha* is recited over each and every type of food.

Chazal established the blessing *"Boreh pri ha'etz"* to be recited over tree fruits. Despite the fact that grapes grow on vines and are subject to blessing of *"boreh pri ha'etz,"* that blessing is not recited over wine. Instead, the *Chachamim* instituted a special *bracha* over wine *"Boreh pri haGefen,"* because of wine's great cultural significance as the beverage of choice.

Bread also has great significance and *Chazal* established a special *bracha* to be recited over it. The blessing *"Boreh pri ha'Adama"* is recited over food items that grow in the ground. Bread, however, which is made from wheat that grows in the ground has its own designated *bracha,* "HaMotzi *lechem min ha'aretz"* (Who brings forth bread out from the earth).

DAF 36
ל"ו

מָתַי מְבָרְכִים עַל שֶׁמֶן זַיִת
WHEN OLIVE OIL IS TO BE BLESSED

As noted in the previous *daf,* the *bracha "Boreh pri ha'etz"* is generally recited over fruits that grow on trees. If one asks what *bracha* should be recited over olive oil, it would be logical to reply— *"Boreh pri ha'etz,"* since olive oil is made from olives, which grow on a tree. However, the *Gemara* states that one who drinks olive oil does not recite any *bracha!*

Why? The *brachot* over food are called *"Birkot HaNehenin"* (blessings of enjoyment), as these *brachot* are recited when enjoying food. The *Gemara* states that if one were to drink olive oil without any other food, the olive oil is objectionable to the body and is not enjoyable. Why should a person recite one of the *Birkot HaNehenin* if he has no enjoyment? The *Gemara* relates that during Talmudic times there was a food item called *"Anigron,"* a sore throat remedy made primarily from olive oil. The *Gemara* notes that although the person drinking the *Anigron* does it for medicinal purposes, i.e., to cure his illness and not because he is hungry, nevertheless, he has to recite *"Boreh pri ha'etz,"* since he does benefit from the olive oil.

בְּרְכַּת חֲמֵשֶׁת מִינֵי דָגָן
BLESSINGS OVER FIVE TYPES OF GRAINS

On this *daf* we learn the appropriate *brachot* for various baked goods.

There are five recognized types of grain: a) wheat, b) barley, c) spelt, d) rye, e) oats.

The *bracha* (blessing) *"Boreh minei mezonot"* (Who created various types of satiating foods) is recited before eating food that contains grain. The after-blessing for such foods is *"Al HaMichya"* ("On the sustenance"). This is the practice when the 'grain' is meant to satisfy the hunger of the person eating the food. However, if grain was mixed into foods in order to bind them together (with the grain functioning as glue so that the foods do not fall apart), then no *bracha* is recited over the grain, but rather, over the primary component of that food alone. For example, over hamburger patties into which flour was mixed so that they would not fall apart, the *bracha* *"She'hakol ne'hi'yeh bid'varo"* (at Whose word everything came into existence) is recited.

בְּרָכָה עַל אֹכֶל מְרֻסָּק
BLESSING OVER MASHED FOOD

According to the Gemara, if a foodstuff is mashed its status and its associated blessing is downgraded. For example, *"She'hakol ne'hi'yeh bid'varo"* is recited over applesauce, even though before it was mashed, it would have been proper to recite *"Boreh pri ha'etz"* over the apples from which the sauce was made.

From what point is a food item considered mashed? If the food is so fully transformed that one can no longer discern its original form, it is considered mashed and afforded downgraded status.

The *Gemara* states that date honey is of lesser importance (as it is not the essence of the fruit) and therefore, *"She'hakol ne'hi'yeh bid'varo"* is recited over it, as is the case with other fruits that have been mashed. However, mashed dates still retain their form, and, therefore, the *bracha* over them remains *"Boreh pri ha'etz."*

Cooked Vegetables: If an individual wants to eat raw, uncooked vegetables that people are accustomed to eating only after they have been cooked — e.g., a raw potato — *"She'hakol ne'hi'yeh bid'varo"* should be recited, since people do not customarily eat potatoes in that manner.

עַל אֵיזֶה לֶחֶם לְבָרֵךְ
CHOOSING WHICH BREAD TO BLESS

This *sugiya* (Talmudic discussion) highlights various instances in which a hungry individual has several different foods in front of them from which to choose and does not know which food to bless.

A complete loaf of bread and an incomplete loaf of bread: While waiting and ready to eat, if there were two bread loaves available on the table — a whole loaf and a sliced loaf — the blessing is to be recited over the whole loaf, because it is of greater prestige. The ruling regarding all foods calls for blessing the whole, uncut food item, when there is one.

Wheat bread and barley bread: If one sits in front of two loaves of bread, e.g., one made from wheat and the other made from barley, it is the wheat loaf that should be blessed. Why? Because wheat precedes barley in the list of the *shiv'at ha'minim* (the seven species of the *Eretz Yisrael*) and is therefore of higher status. As it is written in *Parashat Eikev*: "A land of wheat and barley," — wheat comes before barley.

Various types of bread: What is the ruling if an individual has slices of wheat bread in front of him, along with a whole loaf of barley bread? On one hand, it seems most fitting to recite the blessing over the whole loaf; on the other hand, it also seems appropriate to recite the blessing over the wheat bread. In the aforementioned case, the *Gemara* rules that one ought to hold both breads in hand while reciting the blessing.

WHAT KIND OF OLIVE

For many halachic purposed, the minimal threshold for a food item is a *"k'zayit,"* or an olive's bulk. But what kind of olive does the halacha have in mind? The *Mishnah* in *Masechet Keilim* (17:8) explains: "The olive that the rabbis spoke of is neither the small olive nor the large olive, but rather the medium olive known as the Aguri olive." Rabbi Abahu explained that it was called the *"Aguri"* olive because its oil is gathered (*agur*) within it – i.e. its oil is not absorbed in the meat of the fruit as are the juices of apples or berries, but rather is collected in the fruit.

Translation

טול ... *Tohl...* **Take**

ברוך ... *Baroch...* **Recite a blessing**

Explanation

One who made the blessing over bread and - before personally taking a bite from the bread - verbally instructs others to take pieces from the sliced loaf, need not repeat the blessing. Why? Since his speech directly relates to the meal it does not constitute a *"hesfek,"* or unlawful break between the blessing and the act of eating.

FROM THE TALMUD
Seder Zera'im
Masechet Berachot
DAF 40A

מן התלמוד:
סדר זרעים
מסכת ברכות
דף מ' .

"אמר רב
טול ברוך
טול ברוך
אינו צריך לברך".

הַאֲכָלַת בַּעַל חַיִּים
FEEDING ANIMALS

Feeding of ba'alei chayim (animals): The *Gemara* records the teaching of Rav Yehudah who said in the name of Rav that one who has animals in their possession is prohibited to eat before giving food to those animals. Rav derived this interpretation from the verse in *K'riyat Shema* — *"V'na'ta'ti e'sev ba'sadeh l've'hem'techa, v'achalta v'sa'va'ta"* (And you shall give the grass of the field to your animals, and eat and be satisfied). Note: The feeding of the animals is cited first *("V'na'ta'ti e'sev ba'sadeh l've'hem'techa)* and only after that is *"V'achalta, v'sa'va'ta"* (and you shall eat and be satisfied), where food for a person is mentioned. Therefore, the first obligation of an animal owner is to provide food for the animals in their care, and only afterward to eat themselves.

Dipping of a piece of "HaMotzi" bread in salt: The first piece of bread a person eats after reciting the **HaMotzi** blessing is to be dipped in salt, in order to make tasty the bread of blessing.

A blessing recited in error: One who made a mistake and blessed *"Boreh pri ha'etz"* (Creator of the fruit of the tree) over a fruit that grew in the ground has not fulfilled their religious obligation. For example, one who blessed *"Boreh pri ha'etz"* over a cucumber has not fulfilled the obligation to properly bless God for the food because cucumbers do not grow on trees.

שִׁבְעַת הַמִּינִים
THE SEVEN SPECIES

תְּמָרִים זֵיתִים רִמּוֹן תְּאֵנָה עֲנָבִים שְׂעוֹרָה חִיטָה

We learn in *Sefer Devarim* (Deuteronomy 8:8) that *Eretz Yisrael* is blessed with seven praiseworthy species — "*Eretz* (a land of) wheat *(chee'tah)*, barley *(se'o'rah)*, grapes *(gefen)*, figs *(t'ay'nah)*, pomegranates *(rimon)*, eretz olives *(zayit)*, and honey *(devash)* -- the 'honey' in the Torah refers to *t'marim* date honey.

The *Gemara* says that the seven species listed above are more important than all other fruits and that even within the seven species there are some fruits that are more significant than the rest.

How do we know which type is more important? When one reads the verse above slowly, one notices the phrase "*a land of*" appears twice — "a land of (*'eretz'*) wheat, barley, grapes; figs, pomegranates" and "a land of (*'eretz'*) olives, and honey." The *Gemara* states that the fruits cited in closest proximity to the word '*eretz*' are preferred over fruits that are further from the word "*eretz.*" As such, one who wishes to eat a *t'ay'nah* and a *tamar* (date) should recite the blessing over the *tamar* since it is listed second after the second '*eretz*' and the *t'ay'nah* is listed fourth after the first '*eretz.*'

דְּבָרִים שֶׁצָּרִיךְ לַעֲשׂוֹת מִיָּד
THINGS THAT MUST IMMEDIATELY FOLLOW EACH OTHER

Rav Hiyya Bar Ashi said in the name of Rav that there are three things that must be done immediately following their preparation, without pause:

1) *Techef l's'micha, shechita:* immediately following the owner of the sacrifice's laying of his hands on the head of the sacrificial animal, it must be ritually slaughtered without undo pause.

2) *Techef l'geulah, tefilla:* immediately following the *Birkat Geulah* [blessing of redemption] recited after the *Shema,* the *Amidah* prayer is commenced without waiting.

3) *Techef l'netilat yadayim, bracha:* immediately following "*mayim achronim*" [ritual hand washing after the meal], *Birkat HaMazon* [Grace after Meals] is recited, without stopping to eat or speak between the two.

Abaye added, *Techef l'talmidei chachamim, bracha:* immediately after a householder hosts and takes care of a Torah scholar, a blessing rests upon that home.

Rav Yehudah said: "One who goes out to gardens and groves during the month of *Nissan* and sees trees budding and flourishing should recite *birkat ha'ilanot* (blessing of the trees) - *"Baruch Atah HaShem ... shelo chee'ser b'olamo k'loom u'vara vo b'riyot tovot v'ilanot tovim."* (Blessed are You God ...Who left nothing at all lacking in His world and created good creatures and good trees in it.

Birkat Ha'rei'ach (Blessing of the Scent): When one smells a good and pleasant scent, one should bless God. There are several categories of "good scents." One who smells fragrant grass should recite: *"Baruch Atah HaShem ... Boreh ees'vei besamim"* (Blessed are You, God, creator of fragrant grass.) One who takes the branch of a tree in his hand to inhale its fragrance should recite: *"Baruch Atah HaShem ... Boreh atzei besamim"* (Blessed are You, God, creator of fragrant trees.) One who takes a pleasantly fragrant fruit in his hand in order to sniff it would recite: *"Baruch Atah HaShem ... Ha'noten rei'ach tov l'peirot"* (Blessed are You, God, Who gives good fragrance to fruits.) Over the good scent of an item that does not grow from the ground, *"Boreh mee'nei besamim"* (... Creator of fragrant things) is recited.

One who desires to eat foodstuffs primarily made from one of the five grain-based types of flour (wheat, barley, spelt, rye, oats) recites the blessing *"Boreh mee'nei mezonot"* (Who created various types of foodstuffs) — with the exception of bread, which has its own dedicated blessing, as we learned previously.

After eating food primarily made from one of the five grains, one would bless — *"Baruch Atah HaShem…"* (Blessed are You, God …) *ahl ha'mich'yah ve'ahl ha'kal'kalah* (for the sustenance and the nourishment) *ve'ahl tenuvat ha'sadeh,* (and for the produce of the field) *ve'ahl eretz chemdah tovah* (and for the precious, good land) … *ve'nodeh Lecha ahl ha'aretz ve'ahl ha'michya"* (and we offer thanks to You for the land and for the sustenance).

"Bracha Achrona" (after-blessing) is only recited if one ate the requisite minimum measure (*"shiur"*) of a *k'zayit,* or olive's bulk. The after-blessing for grain-based, non-bread products is known as *"birkat me'ayn shalosh"* (three-faceted blessing), and was given this name because it is effectively a condensed version of the three primary blessings of the major Grace after Meals reciting after bread.

If one eats a fruit from one of *sheev'aht ha'meenim* (the seven species of fruits of *Eretz Yisrael*), the pre-blessing is *"Boreh pri ha'etz."* The after-blessing is: *"Baruch Atah HaShem…"* (Blessed are You, God …) *ahl ha'etz ve'ahl ha'pri ha'etz* (for the tree and the fruit of the tree) *ve'ahl tenuvat ha'sadeh,* (and for the produce of the field). One completes the blessing with the *chatima* (concluding expression) *"Baruch Atah HaShem, ahl ha'etz ve'ahl pri ha'etz."*

Upon eating fruit of one of the *sheev'aht ha'meenim* that physically grew in *Eretz Yisrael,* one completes the after-blessing with the *chatima: "Baruch Atah HaShem, ahl ha'Aretz ve'ahl pei'ro'te'ha"* (Blessed are You, God, for [giving us] the Land and for its fruits).

עַל הַמִּחְיָה
וְעַל
הַכַּלְכָּלָה ...

עַל הַגֶּפֶן
וְעַל פְּרִי...
הַגֶּפֶן

עַל הָעֵץ
וְעַל פְּרִי
הָעֵץ ...

פרק ז'
שְׁלֹשָׁה שֶׁאָכְלוּ

שְׁלֹשָׁה אֲנָשִׁים שֶׁסָּעֲדוּ יַחַד
THREE INDIVIDUALS WHO DINED TOGETHER

Three individuals who dined together and ate bread should convene a *zimun* (invitation to a communal recitation of *Birkat HaMazon*). How is this done? One of the diners invites the others by saying: "*Nevarech she'achalnu mi'Shelo*" (Let us bless Him, from Whose [food] we have eaten) and the fellow diners respond: "*Baruch she'achalnu mi'Shelo, u'v'Tuvo cha'yee'nu*" (Blessed is He, whose food we have eaten and through Whose goodness we live.)

Today, it is customary for the *mezamen* (person who calls for the *zimmun*) to begin by saying: "*Rabotai!* (or *Chaverai!*), *nevarech*" (Gentlemen! [or friends!] Let us bless) — to which the fellow diners respond: "*Yehi Shem HaShem mevorach me'atah ve'ad olam*" (May *HaShem's* Name be blessed, from now until eternity).

The *Gemara* says there is a hint in the Torah for the convening of a *zimun*. *Sefer Devarim* 32:3 reads: "*Ki Shem HaShem Ek'rah*" (When I will call out God's Name), "*Havu godel l'Elokeinu*" (come give glory to our God). In other words, "*Ki Shem HaShem Ek'rah*" refers to the *mezamen's* (one who invites the other diners to bless) call in God's name; and then, "*Havu godel l'Elokeinu*," refers to the diners who hear the invitation and reply with their praise of God.

An individual who, though having not personally eaten, hears people conducting a *zimun* should respond: "*Baruch u'mevorach Shemo tamid l'olam va'ed*" (Blessed and praiseworthy is His Name, always, forever and ever). In the *Gemara*, the aforementioned phrase is written "*Baruch u'mevorach*" (Blessed and Praiseworthy), and the *Ba'alei HaTosafot* commentators and the *Shulchan Arukh* later present the version "*Baruch Hu u'mevorach*" (Blessed is He and Praiseworthy).

ברוך שאכלנו משלו
ובטובו חיינו

בָּרוּך אַתָּה ה'
BLESSED ARE YOU HASHEM

As a general rule, blessings instituted by the sages begin and conclude with *"Baruch."* For example, the first *bracha* of the *Amidah* prayer that begins with *"Baruch [Atah HaShem] Elokeinu, v'Elokei avoteinu"* (Blessed [are You] our God and God of our ancestors), concludes with *"Baruch [Atah HaShem] Magen Avraham"* (Blessed [are You] protector of Abraham).

Although, we notice that the second *bracha* of the *Amidah* prayer, *birkat "Mechaye HaMeitim"* (Who gives life to the dead), does not begin with the word *"Baruch,"* but rather, starts with the words *"Atah Gibor"* (You are mighty). Why?

The *Gemara* explains that a *"bracha ha'smoocha l'chaverta"* (a blessing immediately followed by another blessing) does not begin with *"Baruch"* — meaning, when several *brachot* are recited together as one unified prayer, the *"Baruch"* of the first *bracha* is considered connected to all of the following *brachot*. Such is true in our case, the *"Baruch"* of the first *bracha* serves as the *"Baruch"* for the *brachot* immediately following it in the *Amidah* prayer.

Brachot over food do not conclude with *"Baruch."* For example — The blessing *"Baruch Atah HaShem ... she'hakol ni'hi'yeh bi'D'varo"* (Blessed are You, God ... at whose word all came to be.) Likewise, blessings over *mitzvot* do not conclude with *"Baruch"* — e.g. the *bracha* over *arba'at haminim* (the four species), *"Baruch Atah HaShem ... ahl netilat lulav"* (Blessed are You, God ... on waving of the palm branches) does not conclude with *"Baruch."* Why? Because these blessings are short, one-line blessings, it is unnecessary for them to feature a formal conclusion.

FROM THE TALMUD
SEDER ZERA'IM
MASECHET BERACHOT
DAF 47B

מן התלמוד:
סדר זרעים
מסכת ברכות
דף מ״ז:

"אמר רב
טול ברוך
טול ברוך
אינו צריך לברך".

Translation

טול ... *Tohl* .... **Take**

ברוך ... *Barokh* .. **Bless**

Explanation

The Samaritans (Kutim) were not meticulously observant of all mitzvot, Yet, any commandment which the Samaritans did preserve, they were more punctilious its performance than were their Jewish contemporaries.

כָּךְ עוֹנִים אָמֵן
HOW AMEN IS TO BE SAID

This *sugiya* (Talmudic discussion) deals with *halachot* pertaining to the liturgical response *"Amen."*

What is the meaning of the word *"Amen"*? Three possible interpretations: a) truth b) if only c) truth and if only. As a response to a blessing of praise, "Amen" is an acknowledgment of the truth of the blessing. As a response to a blessing of supplication, "Amen" means *Hale'vai she'habakasha teet'ka'yem* (if only the request will be fulfilled). As a response to a blessing that mixes praise and supplication, "Amen" is represents both "truth" and "if only."

The *Gemara* says one should **not** respond with an *"Amen Chatufa"* ('kidnapped' or abbreviated); or an *"Amen Ketufa"* (truncated); or an *"Amen Yetoma"* (orphaned).

For example:

חטופה   **"Amen Chatufa"**: in which the first syllable is not properly enunciated, or where the Amen response precedes the conclusion of the *bracha*.

קטופה   **"Amen Ketufa"** (truncated), in which the second syllable is not properly enunciated or swallowed (e.g. "A-me").

יתומה   **"Amen Yetoma"** (orphaned), answered with a delay, not immediately following the end of the *bracha,* or when the respondent is unaware of the *bracha* to which s/he is responding.

The obligation to recite the first three *brachot* (blessings) of *Birkat HaMazon* (Grace After Meals) is considered Torah Law. Who fixed the text of these *brachot*?

הַזָּן אֶת הָעוֹלָם

Rav Nachman said that when our ancestors wandered in the desert and God brought Manna down from the Heavens, Moshe Rabbeinu established the *nusach* (formula) of the first *bracha*: *"Baruch Atah … HaZahn et ha'olam" (Blessed are You … who provides sustenance for the world).*

נוֹדֶה לְךָ

After *B'nai Yisrael* entered *Eretz Yisrael*, Yehoshua Bin Nun established the formula for the second *bracha*, *"Nodeh Lecha"* (we give thanks to You).

רַחֵם-נָא ה׳

Several centuries later, King David established the formula for the first half of the third *bracha*: *"Rachem-na HaShem Elokeynu … (Have mercy on us, HaShem, our God …)* up until *"ahl malchut Beit David meshi'checha"* (on the Kingdom of David, your anointed one). When King Solomon, David's son built the *Beit HaMikdash,* he added the second half to the *"Rachem"* (Mercy) *bracha* — *"ve'ahl habayit hagadol v'ha'kadosh … Baruch Atah HaShem, Boneh be'rachamav Yerushalayim. Amen"* ("and over the great and holy house … Blessed are You, *HaShem,* Who in His mercy builds Jerusalem, Amen).

בּוֹנֶה בְּרַחֲמָיו יְרוּשָׁלַיִם

More than a millennium later, after the Bar Kokhba Rebellion and the miraculous recovery of the corpses of martyrs, the sages added the fourth *bracha*: *"Baruch Atah … Hatov V'ha-maitiv"* (Blessed are You … Who is good and has done good for us).

הַטּוֹב וְהַמֵּטִיב

What must be done if, while praying on *Rosh Chodesh,* one realizes only after the conclusion of the Amidah that one forgot to recite *"Ya'aleh v'Yavo"?*

The *Gemara* states, one who forgets to recite *"Ya'aleh v'Yavo"* in *Birkat HaMazon* (Grace After Meals) is not required to go back and repeat the prayer a second time for the sake of including the special *Rosh Chodesh* insertion. However, an individual who neglects to recite *"Ya'aleh v'Yavo"* in the *Shacharit* or *Mincha* services is required to go back and repeat that Amidah. (One who forgets to recite *"Ya'aleh v'Yavo"* during the evening *Arvit* service is not required to repeat those prayers, as we do not sanctify the arrival of the new month at night.)

Why the halachic difference between the Amidah and Birkat HaMazon? Answer: The recitation of the *Amidah* prayer is a *chova* (mandatory obligation). Since the *"Ya'aleh v'Yavo"* prayer is part of the *Amidah* for *Rosh Chodesh,* an individual who neglected to recite *"Ya'aleh v'Yavo"* has not fulfilled their daily obligation and is required to go back and pray again.

In contrast, on *Rosh Chodesh,* there is no *chiyuv* (obligation) to have a *seudah* (festive meal). Only one who feasts is required to recite *"Ya'aleh v'Yavo"* in *Birkat HaMazon.* In any case, recitation of *"Ya'aleh v'Yavo"* in *Birkat HaMazon* is not considered a *Rosh Chodesh* "obligation" and therefore, one who forgets to add that prayer in *Birkat HaMazon* does not go back and repeat that prayer.

Chazal cite several instructions regarding how to treat bread.

❑ One should not pass a cup filled with liquid over bread, lest the liquid spill and cause the bread to get wet and become unpalatable.
❑ One should not throw bread from one place to another.
❑ One should not lean pots filled with food on top of bread, if that food might spill on to the bread and render the bread no longer fit to eat.

Bread is not the only food that is prohibited to throw. It is prohibited to throw any food item that would become spoiled as a result of having been thrown. However, it is permissible to throw edible items that when thrown are not ruined — e.g. nuts with a thick shell. Indeed, the *Gemara* mentions that it was customary to throw nuts in honor of bridegrooms. However, the custom of throwing nuts was not done in the winter, lest the nuts fall and become dirty in the mud, and as a result, could not be eaten.

פֶּרֶק ח׳
אֵלוּ דְבָרִים

Translation

כוס מלא ... *Kos ma'leh* .... **A full cup**

נחלה ... *Nachala* ... **An inheritance**

בלי מצרים ... *B'li meitzarim* ... **Without limitations**

Explanation

One who recites Grace after Meals over a cup of wine (*Kos shel Berachah*) is rewarded with a boundless inheritance.

FROM THE TALMUD
SEDER ZERA'IM
MASECHET BERACHOT
DAF 51A

מִן הַתַּלְמוּד:
סדר זרעים
מסכת ברכות
דף נ״א.

״אמר רבי יוחנן
כל המברך על כוס מלא
נותנין לו
נחלה בלי מצרים״.

DAF 51
נ״א

בִּרְכוֹת הַקִּדּוּשׁ
THE KIDDUSH BLESSING (OVER WINE)

Two blessings were instituted by the sages for the Sabbath evening *Kiddush*: 1) "*Baruch Atah, HaShem* (Blessed are You) … *Boreh pri haGafen* (Creator of the fruit of the vine)" and 2) "*Baruch Atah HaShem* (Blessed are You, God) … *Mekadesh haShabbat*" (Who sanctifies the Sabbath)".

The *Mishnah* presents the opposing view of *Beit Shammai* (School of Shammai) that one must first bless "*Baruch Atah HaShem … Mekadesh haShabbat,*" followed by "*Boreh pri haGafen.*" They reason that if there were no Shabbat, there would be nothing to sanctify, and therefore, it is fitting to bless the Shabbat first.

Beit Hillel disagrees with *Beit Shammai* and contends that first one should bless "*Boreh pri haGafen,*" which is indeed customarily done. *Beit Hillel* explains that without wine, it would be impossible to make Kiddush. For that reason, the *bracha* over the wine should precede the *bracha* sanctifying Shabbat. Moreover, the *bracha* "*Boreh pri haGafen*" is *tadir* (frequent, i.e., recited whenever wine is consumed); while Kiddush is recited only once each week) — as we learned earlier (on *daf 27*): "*Tadir v'she'ayno tadir — tadir kodem*" ([When there is] a Frequent [action, *mitzvah*, occurrence] and an infrequent [action, *mitzvah*, occurrence] — the frequent [is performed] first."

One should taste the wine following the recitation of the *Kiddush* blessing on Shabbat eve and after *Havdalah* at the conclusion of Shabbat.

The *Gemara* states that *Kiddush* and *Havdalah* must be recited using a cup from which no one drank. As such, after someone drank from the cup over which Kiddush or *Havdalah* had been recited, one should not use that same cup for *Kiddush* or *Havdalah* again until after it has been washed.

We learn an additional *halacha* on this *daf* — Mayim Achronim (literally final water, or the custom of ritual washing before *Birkat HaMazon*). These waters are referred to as "*Mayim Achronim,*" to contrast them with the waters used at the beginning of the meal before eating bread. If the water used for *Mayim Achronim* is likely to spill on the table, it is proper to remove any bread resting on the table, so that the water does not spoil it. However, if little crumbs of bread remain, it is not required for them to be removed — though some *halachic* books state that one should also exercise proper caution with the honor of little morsels of bread too.

Rabba Bar Bar Hana was travelling with a caravan. In the midst of the journey, he ate and forgot to recite *Birkat HaMazon.* He truly wanted to return to the location where he ate in order to recite the blessings there. However, he knew that even if he were to politely ask the members of the caravan to wait for him, they would not agree. Therefore, since fulfilling the *mitzvot* was as important as gold in his eyes — a tremendous quantity of gold, at that — Rabba Bar Bar Hana told the members of the caravan: "I must return to the place where I ate, as I forgot gold there!" To him, the fulfillment of *mitzvot* was worth more than gold.

The *Gemara* relates that the caravan members agreed. Rabba Bar Bar Hana returned to the spot where he ate, so that he could there recite *Birkat HaMazon.* He arrived at the location and indeed recited *Birkat HaMazon* — then, a miracle occurred on his behalf! He found a large piece of gold jewelry in the shape of a dove.

Why did God specifically send Rabba Bar Bar Hana gold in the shape of a dove? The *Gemara* answers that a dove was chosen because *Am Yisrael* is likened to a dove. How so? Just as a dove escapes from its enemies solely by use of its wings which allow the bird to soar high above its foes, so, too, the merit of *mitzvot* fulfilled by Jews protects them from their enemies.

פרק ט׳
הָרוֹאֶה

בִּרְכַּת הַגּוֹמֵל
BLESSING OF THANKSGIVING

One who experiences an earthquake or one who hears thunder immediately recites: *"Baruch Atah HaShem … she'Kocho u'Gevurato maleh olam"* (Blessed are You HaShem … Whose strength and power fill the world.)

שֶׁהֶחֱיָנוּ וְקִיְּמָנוּ וְהִגִּיעָנוּ לִזְמַן הַזֶּה

One who builds a new home or acquires new tools or utensils and is pleased with them, recites: *"Baruch Atah HaShem … she'he'cheiyanu, v'ki'ye'manu, v'higi'anu la'z'man ha'zeh"* (Blessed are You, God … Who has granted us life and sustained us and enabled us to reach this occasion.)

The *Gemara* lists four groups of people who need to recite *Birkat HaGomel* (Blessing of Thanksgiving): a) One who sailed across the ocean and reached dry land, b) one who walked in the desert and reached an inhabited area, c) one survived a gravely serious illness, and d) one who was released from incarceration.

שֶׁגְּמָלַנִי כָּל טוֹב, הַגּוֹמֵל לְחַיָּבִים טוֹבוֹת

Birkat HaGomel is to be recited in the presence of a *tzibbur* (congregation) of ten. The person reciting *Birkat HaGomel* says: *"Baruch Atah HaShem … (Blessed are You, God …) HaGomel l'chayavim tovot, she'g'malani (kol) tov"* (Who rewards the undeserving with goodness, He has bestowed (every) goodness upon me.) And the *tzibbur* responds: *"Mi She'gam'lecha (kol) tov, Hu ye'ga'melcha kol tov, selah."* (May He who rewarded you with all goodness, reward you with all goodness forever.)

אָמֵן!
מִי שֶׁגְּמָלְךָ כָּל טוֹב
כָּל טוֹב הוּא יִגְמָלְךָ
סֶלָה

בְּצַלְאֵל = בְּצֵל אֵ־ל
IN THE SHADOW OF GOD

Rav Shmuel Bar Nachmani taught in the name of Rabbi Yonatan: Betzalel, chief architect of the *Mishkan* (Tabernacle) and its vessels, was named on account of his wisdom. How was his wisdom revealed? When God commanded Moshe Rabbeinu to build the *Mishkan*, God told Moshe to make the *Mishkan* first, and only afterward to construct the ark and other sacred vessels. Despite the sequence of God's instruction, Moshe directed Betzalel to build in the reverse order — first the vessels and afterward the *Mishkan* itself.

Betzalel questioned Moshe, saying: "The standard process in the world is for a person to build a house and then place the vessels inside. People do not customarily place down vessels and build a house around them." Moshe Rabbeinu replied: "You are wise! How did you know that God actually instructed me to build the *Mishkan* first and the vessels afterward? Perhaps you were *Be'tzel-El* (in God's shadow) and you heard that He commanded me to build the *Mishkan* first and attend to the vessels afterward?! That is why you were called "Betzalel".

חֲלוֹמוֹת הַלַּיְלָה
DREAMS

Rav Shmuel Bar Nachmani taught in the name of Rabbi Yonatan: Generally one dreams at night about the same things that occupied one's mind and thoughts over the course of the day. The *Gemara* tells of a Roman emperor who said to Rabbi Yehoshua ben Chananya: "You Jews say that you are extremely wise. If so, tell me please what I will dream tonight. Rabbi Yehoshua ben Chananya replied: "You will dream that your enemies enslave you and force you into hard labor. They will belittle you and humiliate you." The emperor thought all day about the images Rabbi Yehoshua described to him. That night, the emperor suffered a nightmare in which he saw dreamed that his enemies tortured and humiliated him.

King Shapur of Persia approached Shmuel and likewise said: "You Jews claim you are extremely wise. If that is so, tell me what I will see in my dream tonight." Shmuel replied: "You will dream that the Romans come and take you into captivity. They will force you to grind date pits in the gold mills." Shapur thought the entire day about the images Shmuel had described and at night he was indeed visited by those terror-filled dreams.

בְּרָכוֹת בְּעֵת בִּקּוּר בְּבָבֶל
BLESSINGS DURING A VISIT TO BABYLONIA

The Babylonians destroyed the First *Beit HaMikdash*. On this *daf,* we learn several about blessings instituted by the *Chachamim* to be recited upon seeing historical sites. Rav Hamnuna taught: One who arrives in *Bavel* (Babylonia) must recite five *brachot* (blessings). Among these *brachot* is a *bracha* on seeing the city of Babylon, the capital of Bavel.

One who saw the ancient city of Bavel was to recite: *"Baruch she'He'che'reev Bavel ha'rasha"* (Blessed is the One Who destroyed the wicked Babylon); Bavel had been a great kingdom, but God punished them and so the city was destroyed. One who saw the ruins of the house of King Nevuchadnezzar was to recite: *"Baruch she'Hechreev et bey'to shel Nevuchadnezzar ha'rasha"* (Blessed in the One Who destroyed the house of the wicked Nevuchadnezzar).

One who saw the lion's den into which Daniel was thrown (see Daniel Chapter 6) and in which God safeguarded Daniel from the voracious lions, blesses: *"Baruch She'Asah" nissim l'Avoteinu bamakom hazeh"* (Blessed is the One Who performed miracles for our ancestors in this place.)

In addition, one who saw the furnace into which Hananiah, Mishael, and Azariah were thrown, and from which God rescued them, recites the same abovementioned *bracha*. One who saw fields in Bavel, which were unfit for planting because God punished the local population [by making their fields unfit for planting], was to recite: *"Baruch Omer v'Oseh, Gozer u'Mekayem,"* (Blessed is the One Who Speaks and Acts, Decrees and Fulfills).

RABBI AND ANTONINUS

The Divine oracle told Rivka when she was suffering from her pregnancy, "Two nations are in your wombs." The sages offered a homiletic interpretation of the verse. Instead of *"goyim,"* they read *"gay-im,"* meaning proud ones. Yaakov and Eisav were her two children, the progenitors of the Jewish People and the Roman Empire. The two proud ones were the wealthy leading of those respective groups – Rabbi Yehudah Ha-Nasi and the Emperor Antoninus. Their wealth was apparent in that they never lacked from their table cucumber, radish, and horseradish, even during the winter when such vegetables are out of season. Legend has it that Rabbi and Antoninus were good friends, marking a highpoint in the otherwise acrimonious history of Jewish-Roman relations.

Translation

כוס מלא ... *Kos ma'leh* .... **A full cup**

נחלה ... *Nachala* ... **An inheritance**

בלי מצרים ... *B'li meitzarim* ... **Without limitations**

Explanation

A recently deceased person is not forgotten from the hearts of their surviving loved ones until twelve months have passed. Accordingly, the extended period of mourning following the passing of a mother or father lasts twelve months.

מן התלמוד:
סדר זרעים
מסכת ברכות
דף נ"ח:

FROM THE TALMUD
SEDER ZERA'IM
MASECHET BERACHOT
DAF 58B

"אין המת
משתכח מן הלב
אלא
לאחר
שנים עשר חדש".

שֵׁשׁ מֵאוֹת אֶלֶף יְהוּדִים
600,000 JEWS

DAF 58
נ"ח

The *Gemara* says that a Jew who sees a multitude of Israel, (i.e., 600,000 Jews gathered together) should bless God. Each one of these hundreds of thousands of individuals looks and thinks differently, and yet, God knows the inner thoughts of each of them. On such an occasion, the required *bracha* is: *"Baruch Atah HaShem, Elokeinu Melech HaOlam, Chacham HaRazim"* (Blessed are You, *HaShem,* our God, King of the universe, Who Knows all secrets).

One who sees a great Torah scholar recites: *"Baruch Atah ... She'Cha'lak m'Chochmato l'yirai'av"* (Blessed are You ... Who has shared His wisdom with those who revere Him). One who sees a gentile scholar recites: *"Baruch Atah ... she'Natan me'Chochmato l'va'sahr va'dahm"* (Blessed is the One Who gave of His wisdom to flesh and blood).

Upon seeing a Jewish king, one blesses: *"Baruch Atah ... she'Chalak mi'kevodo l'yirai'av"* (Blessed are You ... Who has shared of His glory with those who revere Him.) One who sees a gentile king recites: *"Baruch Atah ... she'Natan mi'kevodo le'vasahr va'dahm"* (Blessed are You ... Who has given of His glory to flesh and blood).

בִּרְכַּת הַחַמָּה
BLESSING OF THE SUN

The sun rises every morning and sets every evening. It revolves in the sky and each year returns to the point at which it began to glow at the time of the creation of the world. However, once every 28 years, the sun returns to its exact original location at the precise moment of the week (Wednesday morning) it was created. One who sees the sun on that special anniversary recites the blessing: *"Baruch Atah, HaShem, Elokeynu Melech HaOlam, Oseh Ma'aseh Breisheet"* (Blessed are you, *HaShem*, our God, King of the universe, Author of creation.)

The *Shehecheyanu* Blessing: The *Gemara* states that one who hears good news, which fills his or her heart with joy blesses God: *"Baruch Atah … Shehecheyanu v'ki'ye'manu v'hi'gi'anu la'z'man ha'zeh"* (Blessed are You … Who has granted us life, sustained us and enabled us to reach this occasion). If those joyous tidings are good for the individual as well as for others, he or she must bless *"Baruch Atah HaShem, Elokeynu Melech HaOlam, HaTov v'ha'Meitiv"* (Blessed are You, *HaShem,* our God, King of the universe, Who is good and does good). If a man is informed that his wife gave birth to a baby boy, he blesses: *"HaTov v'ha'Meitiv,"* since both he and his wife are happy.

THE GREAT SEA

Blessing Upon seeing the Great Sea, one makes a blessing "Blessed are you Hashem… Who made the Great Sea." The commentators debated whether this blessing is specific to the Mediterranean Sea which is the largest body of water near the Land of Israel, or whether it refers to the oceans of the world. A reconciliation of the two views would acknowledge that Mediterranean Sea is itself part of the same large contiguous body of water covering most of the earth as are the various oceans. The *Gemara* teaches that the blessing is only to be recited if one has not seen the Sea in the past thirty days. Why? The natural wonders of the earth make an impression when one does not see them on a regular basis; they make impressions only when seen at intervals.

Rabbi Akiva said: A person should become accustomed to say — *"Kol mah she'HaShem oseh, l'tova Hu oseh"* (Everything God does — He does for the best).

Once, Rabbi Akiva went out on a journey, bringing with him a donkey, a rooster, and a candle. When Akiva reached an inhabited location, he sought out a place to sleep but none would agree to let him enter their home. Rabbi Akiva was left with no choice; he found a place to sleep in a field outside the city. He did not become angry or annoyed, rather, he just said: *"Kol mah she'HaShem oseh, l'tova Hu oseh."*

Suddenly, in the middle of the night, some strange things occurred. A wind began to blow and extinguished the candle. A cat passed by and consumed the rooster. Worst of all — a lion came and devoured the donkey. Rabbi Akiva was left alone, without anything at all, in the dark. Yet, he still said: *"Kol mah she'HaShem oseh, l'tova Hu oseh."*

Some time later, Rabbi Akiva heard a series of extremely loud noises. A large band of soldiers attacked the city and took all of it citizens hostage. Rabbi Akiva viewed these events as proof that everything God does is for the best. Had he been in the city, or had his candle been visible, or his animals noisy Akiva would have been caught and taken into captivity. Seemingly detrimental experiences turned out, in hindsight, to have saved him.

מְשַׁל הַדָּגִים
PARABLE OF THE FISH

DAF 61
ס"א

Once, the Roman government issued a decree prohibiting Jews from occupying themselves with Torah study. Rabbi Akiva did not obey the decree. Rather, he continued to teach his students Torah, without fear. Pappos ben Yehudah found Rabbi Akiva convening a large pubic assembly for Torah study. Pappos questioned him: Do you not fear the empire?

Akiva replied: "Allow me to share a parable with you. To what can this situation be compared? It is like a fox walking along the riverbank who saw fish quickly fleeing. The fox asked them: 'From whom are you fleeing?' The fish responded: 'We are fleeing from the nets of the fisherman who are trying to hunt us.' The fox replied: 'Come, dear fish. Come up on the dry land and we will reside together!' The fish told the fox, 'your proposal is not clever, and is even foolish. If we were afraid in the water — which is our natural habitat — all the more so would we be in fear outside the water, as fish out of water — die!'"

Rabbi Akiva concluded by telling Pappos Ben Yehudah, "For a Jew, the Torah is like water; it is his life. How is it possible to consider refraining from Torah study?"

קַפָּנְדַּרְיָא — קִצּוּר דֶּרֶךְ
KAPPANDARYA — A SHORTCUT

When the *Beit HaMikdash* stood, Jews were bidden to ascend to *Har HaBayit* (Temple Mount) in Jerusalem. On this *daf,* we learn that it was prohibited to enter *Har HaBayit* in a disrespectful manner. As such, one was prohibited to enter *Har HaBayit* while carrying a walking stick and one was required to remove one's shoes, as signs of respect for the holiest place in the world.

Due to the sanctity of the *Beit HaMikdash*, it was also prohibited to take a shortcut through *Har Habayit.* 'Kappandarya' is an Aramaic word, which translates as 'shortcut." It is prohibited to cross through *Har HaBayit* to shorten one's journey. Rather, one was required to circle around *Har HaBayit.* The Gemara applies this *Kappandarya* rule to synagogues too. If a synagogue has two entrances, it is prohibited to enter through one set of doors and exit through the other. However, an individual who enters the synagogue through one door to pray is permitted to exit through a second door, since he clearly did not enter the synagogue as a shortcut, but rather for the legitimate purpose of prayer.

כְּבוֹד תַּלְמִידֵי חֲכָמִים
HONOR OF TORAH SCHOLARS

When the academy for Torah Scholars was established in Yavneh, the holy *Tannaim* Rabbi Yehudah, Rabbi Yossi, Rabbi Nechemiah and Rabbi Elazar Ben Rabbi Yossi HaGlili assembled and offered *drashot* (sermons) in honor of those who hosted yeshiva students in their homes

Rabbi Yehudah presented the following sermon: It is written in the Torah that an Egyptian is permitted to convert and become a Jew. While we know the Egyptians tortured our ancestors in Egypt, they are not prohibited from joining the Jewish people because they were hospitable to our forefather Ya'akov and his family when they arrived in Egypt during the famine. Rabbi Yehudah asserted that the Egyptians did not receive Ya'akov Avinu and his sons because they aspired to observe the mitzvah of *Hachnassat Orchim* (hospitality, welcoming guests), but rather because they sought to derive material benefit from the Israelite presence in Egypt. Nevertheless, the merit of that good deed stood in their favor to allow them to convert. Likewise, those who host a *talmid chacham,* feed him and provide him with drink, expressly in order to fulfill the mitzvah of *hachanassat orchim*, certainly merit a huge reward.

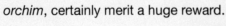

מַעֲלַת תַּלְמִיד חָכָם
THE LOFTY STATUES OF A TORAH SCHOLAR

Rabbi Avin HaLevi said the status of a *talmid chacham* (Torah scholar) is so great that a *seudah* (meal) in which a *talmid chacham* participates is automatically an important *seudah*. Concerning the *seudah* shared by Yitro (Moshe's father-in-law), Aharon HaKohen, and the elders of Israel, it is said the feast took place "before God," i.e., that the meal enjoyed the radiant splendor of the Divine Presence, owing to the participation of the righteous of the generation.

Rabbi Avin HaLevi also taught that when bidding farewell to an individual who is about to depart, one should say, "Lech l'shalom" (Go *to* peace – and not "lech **b'**shalom" go *in* peace). Only when one bids farewell to a deceased person at their funeral should one say, *"Lech b'shalom."*

Rabbi Levi Bar Hiyya taught that it is fitting to juxtapose the performance of *mitzvot*. For example, one should learn Torah and pray immediately afterward. One who does so merits great reward in the world-to-come.

B'Sha'ah – Tova
We complete learning *Masechet Berachot!*

Please join us in learning OTHER *Masechtot*

הדרן עלך מסכת ברכות
Hadran Alakh Masechet Berachot
We will return to you Tractate Berachot
[We learned from you, and we will return to learn from you again.]

Please take a look at the sample
of our weekly publications on the
following four pages.
Enjoy!

For more information,
please contact:
Yael Schulman,
Director, Daf Yomi for US

yael@talmudisraeli.co.il

בס"ד

Weekly Kit 159 – Parashat Noach
Seder Nezikin | Bava Metzia, Daf 34-40 | 28 Tishrei – 4 Cheshvan (Oct. 30 - Nov. 5)

Daf 34: הַקִּנְיָן שֶׁיָּחוּל לְאַחַר זְמָן – An Acquisition that Takes Effect Following a Predetermined Delay

An individual who wants to acquire a particular item must take action to do so. One may acquire a chair by **lifting it**. As a result of lifting the chair, its ownership is transferred from the seller to the buyer. One of the methods of acquiring cattle is by **pulling it,** e.g., tugging on its harness and causing the animal to move from the place it was standing.

It is insufficient for the buyer and seller to verbally agree that they both want the acquisition to occur. **As long as no act of acquisition has taken place, no change of ownership has occurred.**

Once, an individual sought to arrange an acquisition in an unusual manner: He owned a chess set that he wanted to sell. When a potential buyer came to acquire the set, the seller said: "Although I want to sell this chess set, I want to do so **one week from today,** since I would still like to use it this week."

What do we do in such a case? Do we delay the act of acquisition until the week has passed? On this *daf* we learn that the act of acquisition need not wait. **The act of acquisition may be done today, along with a statement: "We stipulate the acquisition will take place one week from today."**

Daf 35: "הַמַּפְקִיד" וְ"שׁוֹמֵר פִּקָּדוֹן" – The Depositor and The Guardian of a Deposited Possession

The chapter we are learning is called *"HaMafkid."* A *mafkid* is a person who deposits an item with someone in order for it to be safeguarded. The owner of the object is known in the Talmud as **"HaMafkid,"** and the person who received the object to watch over, is called **"Shomer"** or **"Shomer Pikadon,"** the watchperson or guardian of a deposited item.

An individual who takes responsibility for watching over an object is required to guard it. If one neglects to do so, and the object becomes damaged or stolen, that person is liable to repay the value of the object to the owner.

One of the different types of guardians is a "Shomer Chinam," an unpaid guardian. A *shomer chinam* is a person who has agreed to watch over an object without receiving payment. A *shomer chinam* is not obligated to repay the person who deposited their possession with them if that item is stolen, or lost, or damaged in any way— **unless that *shomer chinam* was negligent in their supervision.**

Scan this QR CODE to view a video clip about this *sugya*

FROM THE TALMUD
SEDER NEZIKIN
MASECHET BAVA METZIA
daf 38

מן התלמוד:
סדר נזיקין, מסכת בבא מציעא, (דף ל"ח)
"אתמר, שבוי שנשבה - רב אמר: אין
מורידין קרוב לנכסיו, שמואל אמר:
מורידין קרוב לנכסיו."

Translation

שיימינן ... *Shaymeenan* ... **We assess (appraise) them**
עובדא ... *Ovda* .... **Occurrence, tale**
מעיילין ... *M'ay'lin* .... **Insert, introduce**

Explanation

If a Jew was taken into captivity by non-Jews, Rav and Shmuel disagree as to whether a relative of that captive may be permitted to take the captive's property and treat it as their own until that relative returns; or are they to leave the property alone, lest it suffer damage.

Talmud Israeli in America

The outstanding Talmud Israeli project is now available in North America! Tens of thousands of copies of Talmud Israeli are distributed weekly across Israel – in schools, synagogues, and communities – earning widespread support from Israel's Ministry of Education. Talmud Israeli brings the teachings of the Talmud to everyone. DAF YOMI FOR US is user-friendly and intended for people of all ages and levels of Talmudic knowledge. We are thrilled to share our program with your school or synagogue and provide you with our weekly booklet. Contact us to sign up for Talmud Israeli – Daf Yomi for US and engage in this one-of-a-kind, new educational experience!

FOUNDER & EDITOR: MEIR JAKOBSOHN | EDUCATIONAL DIRECTOR & EDITOR: RABBI AVI RATH | BOARD CHAIRMAN: HAIM FREILICMAN, C.P.A.
CHAIRMAN, DAF YOMI FOR US: GAL NAOR | תלמוד ישראלי | SPONSORED BY: MEDISON | T: 914-413-3128 | Talmudisraeli@Medison.co.il

1

Daf 36: "שְׁבוּעַת הַפִּקָּדוֹן" – Oath of the Deposited Item

If a *shomer* of a deposited object says to the *mafkid*: *"I took good care of the object. However, thieves came in the middle of the night and stole it. I apologize. I was sound asleep and did not hear them. I am exempt from repaying you for the object, **since a shomer chinam is only liable to repay if s/he was negligent."** That *shomer*

Please guard these sacks! There is gold inside them and thieves are chasing us!

is in fact exempt from payment. However, the Torah stipulates that the *shomer* **must take an oath in a *beit din* that their claim is truthful.**

This oath is called **"Shvu'at HaPikadon,"** oath of the deposited item.

If a *shomer* transgressed and stole guarded items, and also took a false oath, when s/he asks for *teshuva,* the items must be immediately returned to the *mafkid*. In addition, the Torah requires the *shomer* perform a specific order of atonement:

a) Repay the *mafkid* **an additional 1/5 of the value of the object.**

b) Bring a *Korban Asham* (guilt offering) to repent for making a false oath.

Daf 37: מַחְלֹקֶת עַל גֹבַה הַפִּקָּדוֹן –
Dispute Over Collection of a Deposit

Reuven lived in a village near the border. One day, gunshots were heard throughout the village. Reuven immediately hid in the safe room of his house. Peering through a narrow slit in the window, Reuven saw two people running, each one holding a sack. To his complete surprise, the two people entered Reuven's house and said: *"We beg you, please watch over these sacks for us. They contain gold and thieves are chasing after us."* Reuven agreed, and the pair immediately ran off into the forest. The thieves soon lost track of the owners of the sacks. Peace and tranquility prevailed in the village once again.

Just a few days later, the owners of the two sacks reappeared at Reuven's house. They thanked Reuven from the bottom of their hearts for his help. When Reuven brought out the sacks and laid them in front of the gentlemen, an intense dispute erupted. It seems that one sack contained one pound of gold, while the other sack held 2 pounds of gold. Each of the men insisted: **The heavier bag is mine!**

What should Reuven do? Reuven should only give one pound of gold to each of the two men—since both men agree, without question, that they each certainly deserve one pound of gold. The third pound, the one still in dispute, remains in Reuven's possession until Elijah the Prophet arrives to determine which one of the men is correct.

♦ | Made in Israel

Bamba
Manufactured by Osem

Bamba is one of the most popular snack foods in Israel. It is a baked peanut butter puff snack beloved by Israelis of all ages – from babies to adults. Bamba is not only delicious, it is relatively healthy too. It contains no cholesterol, no preservatives and no food coloring and is also vitamin-enriched. In 2008, scientists investigated why Jews in Great Britain have ten times more peanut allergies than Jews in Israel. After researching the situation – it was determined that Bamba was the answer. Infants and children in Israel eat copious amounts of Bamba and thus, peanut allergy is rare.

Thank you, Israeli food manufacturers for making a snack that is not only delicious, but may protect against allergies as well!

Bamba snacks.
Photo Source: Wikipedia
Photos/ Nsaum75

תלמוד ישראלי
לכלנו ✡ Daf Yomi for US

🔲 Daf 38: אַחְרָיוּת הַשּׁוֹמֵר עַל פֵּרוֹת חֲבֵרוֹ –
Liability of a Guardian over the Neighbor's Fruit

These few pages in the Talmud teach about different actions a guardian must take in order to prevent a decrease in value of the deposit under their care. There was a case of a person who took responsibility for watching over a neighbor's fruit. After some time passed, the *shomer* noticed the quality of the produce was unsatisfactory. The fruit was becoming too ripe. If the *shomer* **left the fruit untouched, it would start to decay and the *mafkid* would forfeit any benefit from the produce.**

The *shomer* attempted to locate the *mafkid* in order to ask what to do, but did not succeed. It became clear the *mafkid* was traveling abroad.

What should the *shomer* do with the fruit?

Our Sages say that the *shomer* must approach the *beit din* and tell them exactly what had happened. Then, under the *beit din's* supervision, the *shomer* is directed to sell the produce and safeguard the proceeds for the *mafkid*.

Scan this QR CODE to view a video clip about this *sugya*

🔲 Daf 39: "הַמּוֹצִיא מֵחֲבֵרוֹ - עָלָיו הָרְאָיָה" –
One Who Seeks to Seize Property from a Peer Bears the Burden of Proof

Two people argue over a financial debt. Reuven claims Shimon owes him money, while Shimon insists he does not owe Reuven anything. They must approach the *beit din* to determine who is correct.

How do the judges determine whose claim is correct?

If one of the two parties has proof that he is correct, then the *beit din* accepts his evidence to be true. If Reuven provides witnesses to testify on his behalf that Shimon does indeed owe him money, the *beit din* examines the witnesses to verify their testimony is truthful and then determines that Shimon owes money to Reuven.

What is done if neither party can prove their claim?
In such a case, the court employs a basic principle that states: **one who seeks to seize property from a peer bears the burden of proof.** Meaning, if someone claims they are owed money by another person, s/he is obligated to provide proof of the claim. In the absence of proof, the *beit din* has no basis to obligate the accused to pay.

Scan this QR CODE to view a video clip about this *sugya*

✴ | This Week in Jewish History

On the 30th of Tishrei in 1958, the foundation stone was placed for the new building of the Israeli Parliament, the Knesset. The Knesset has 120 members, the same number at the *Knesset Ha'gedola* of the Second Temple Era. Each Knesset session is known by its election number, i.e., the Knesset elected in Israel's first election in 1949 is known as the First Knesset. The Twentieth Knesset is now in session. The Knesset plenum meets on Mondays, Tuesdays and Wednesdays. There are 14 standing Knesset Committees that meet regularly and are made up of Knesset Members from different parties. Today, there are 10 parties in the Knesset. The largest parties are Likud, lead by Prime Minister Benjamin Netanyahu, and the Zionist Union, lead by Isaac Herzog.

Israeli Knesset Building in Jerusalem.
TOP: Photo Source: Israel Government Press Office
BOTTOM: Photo Source: Wikipedia/ Leif Knutsen

Daf 40: רַב הוּנָא – Rav Huna

The *Amora* Rav Huna lived in Babylonia for most of his life and achieved the distinction of being the *Gadol Hador,* the greatest Torah scholar of his generation. Rav Huna's primary teacher and mentor was Rav, who conferred rabbinic ordination upon Rav Huna.

During the same period, Rav served as *Rosh Yeshiva* of Sura and his colleague Shmuel served as *Rosh Yeshiva* of Nehardea. After Rav's death, a new *Rosh Yeshiva* was not immediately appointed in Sura. As a result, students migrated to the yeshiva of Nehardea to learn Torah from Shmuel.

Years later, Shmuel passed on. The city of Nehardea was ravaged by war, making it too difficult to sustain a Yeshiva there. It was at that time, **the Sages of Babylonia decided to appoint Rav Huna as Rosh Yeshiva of Sura. He was a very successful Rosh Yeshiva. Students flocked from all over to learn from Rav Huna. With the passage of time, Rav Huna had 13 people with powerful voices transmitting his teachings to the public.**

The Talmud teaches in *Masechet Ketubot,* that at the end of a *shiur,* when Rav Huna's students shook off their garments as they rose to leave, they raised such a massive cloud of dust that the sky became overcast.

??? QUESTIONS OF THE WEEK
All answers can be found in this Daf Yomi booklet

1. What is the meaning of "Hamotzi michavero, alav ha're'ayah," and when is this principle employed?

2. What should a guardian who is entrusted with supervision over fruit that is beginning to decay do if the owner is unable to retrieve their deposit?

3. What must a person who regrets having stolen an item and giving false testimony do in order to repay the owner for the theft?

Please email answers to questions to
answers@talmudisraeli.co.il
for a chance to win an iPad mini!

📖 | Dvar Torah for the Shabbat Table

It says in *Pirkei Avot* that 10 generations separated between Noah and Abraham. Torah commentators drew extensive comparisons between Noah and Abraham.

In this week's *parasha*, Rashi states: In our *parasha* it is says: "God walked with Noah" and our Patriarch Avraham ascribes almost exactly the same quality to himself, i.e., "God, whom I walked before."

What is the difference between these two verses and the description regarding walking with God? Rashi employs a close reading of the text: **"Noah needed God's aid."** Therefore, the Torah says that "God walked with Noah" to support him. However, our **Patriarch Avraham was empowered and righteously walked on his own.** Therefore, the verse states that Avraham **walked before God.**

👤 | Person of the Week

Israeli combat navigator Ron Arad fell captive in Lebanon and is considered Missing In Action (MIA). He was born in Magdiel, completed flight school and served as a Phantom fighter plane combat navigator. In 1986, Arad set out on a mission to hit terrorist targets in southern Lebanon. A technical malfunction triggered an explosion near the plane, causing its two crew members to abandon the aircraft. Pilot Yishai Aviram was rescued via helicopter. Arad fell captive to the Shiite "AMAL" organization. His captors handed over three letters he wrote, along with one photo. Arad was not allowed any visitors; even representatives of the International Red Cross were not permitted to see him. All attempts to broker a deal to gain Arad's release failed. In 1988, all traces of Arad disappeared. It is suspected Arad was transferred over to another organization, moved to Iran, or killed by his captors. Ron Arad's true fate remains unknown.

4

TALMUD ISRAELI/DAF YOMI FOR US: 112 W. 34th Street, 18th flr. • New York, N.Y. 10120 • www.talmudisraeli.com
YAEL SCHULMAN, Director, yael@talmudisraeli.co.il

Made in the USA
Columbia, SC
04 December 2019